Full Title

Covenants of Promise

THE PURPOSE OF THE MEDIATOR

BY

JON M. LOOSE

HaEtanim

TISHREI15
www.tishrei15.com

The Divine Pattern Collection

HaEtanim
TISHREI15
www.tishrei15.com

Images

Preface

The whole purpose, the telos, of exegesis is to go full circle. You must return to saying what God has said in the Text. Anything less, anything other, invites the ancient question of Hasatan: *Did God really say?* That is the threshold of distortion. Anything else is a monument to oneself, not a witness to the Word. Exegesis ends where it began: with the sacred Text repeated, not re-imagined. The goal is not innovation, but restoration, echoing the utterance with such clarity that the original breath is felt again.

For many, the aspiration to become a theologian is less a calling than a detour—one that tragically bypasses their true vocation as a weatherman, where you have the benefit of being paid for being wrong.

Translation, too, plays its part. One would suppose that a faithful translation would exhibit continuity, would preserve Jeremiah's context, his covenantal vision, his prophetic cadence. But this is not always the case. Translators, like theologians, are not immune to agenda. Have they intended, as the prophet did, to maintain purpose and continuity? Or have they, consciously or not, allowed theological bias to fracture the thread?

What this book attempts to do is to refute the use of theological eisegesis as a hermeneutic, a method that imports foreign categories into sacred text under the guise of interpretation. This is all too common and even has official terms. In the church it is called Magisterium. In Rabbinic Judaism it is called Masorah. Protestants often use the term economy or covenantal as ploy to manage understanding.

Notes

SEMANTICALLY SIMILAR WORDS WILL BE COLOR CODED FOR EASE OF REFERENCE. COLOR CODED WORDS WILL BE IN ALL LANGUAGES;

BROWN FOR COVENANT ; ORANGE FOR THE QUALIFIER WORD FOR COVENANT : BLUE FOR HASHEM : RED FOR CITATIONS

Abbreviations

AH.,	Against Heresies - Irenaeus
art.,	article
DAP.,	The Demonstration of Apostolic Preaching
e.g.,	for example
et al.,	and others
ff.,	following
fn.,	footnote
en.,	end note
Gr.,	Greek (Koine)
Heb.,	Hebrew
ibid.,	the same
i.e.,	that is
infra.,	below
m	Mazoretic Text
ME.,	Middle English
MS.,	manuscript
OE.,	Old English
op. cit.,	in the work cited
p.,	page
pp.,	pages
supra.,	above
sect.,	section
Tr.,	Targum
viz.,	namely

Contents

One

❦

The Prophet Jeremiah

" And if they could talk to one another, don't you think they'd suppose that the names they used applied to the things they see passing before them?" - Plato's Republic

One ever present question would be: Who here could imagine the prophet Jeremiah as a supersessionist?

As Plato remarked, do you suppose that there must be communication between Jeremiah, the translation and us.

"Behold, days are coming," declares the LORD, "when I will cut a new covenant with the house of Israel and the house of Judah, not like the covenant which I cut with their fathers on the day I took them by the hand to bring them out of the land of Egypt, My covenant which they broke, although I was a husband to them," declares the LORD. "For this is the covenant which I will cut with the house of Israel after those days," declares the LORD: "I will put My law within them and write it on their heart; and I will be their God, and they shall be My people. -Jeremiah 31:31-33

This is not merely an ancient utterance; they are the living words of יִרְמְיָהוּ Jeremiah - prophet of Israel, whose voice still reverberates through the sacred architecture of time. The passage is found in Jeremiah 31:31-34, a covenantal declaration that transcends its historical moment, reaching forward with divine intentionality. A proper understanding of what a covenant makes this passage crucial and foundational to our existence in this present day.

This is no isolated oracle, for the very same words reappear, almost verbatim, in Hebrews 8:8–12, a deliberate echo, not accidental. The writer of Hebrews does not paraphrase; he invokes. He draws the thread taut between the prophetic and the apostolic, between Sinai's shadow and the internal inscription of divine law.

This is not theological nostalgia. It is sacred continuity. What Jeremiah foresaw, Hebrews affirms: a covenant not engraved on stone, but etched upon the heart. Not mediated by ritual alone, but by intimacy, by knowing.

His words are not relics. They are living architecture. They belong not only to Israel's past, but to the present tense of divine orchestration. Thus we arrive at the threshold of Hebrews, not as casual readers, but as those summoned to ascend. Here, the veil parts. The earthly gives way to the heavenly. The text does not merely speak; it ministers. Hebrews is no epistolary afterthought—it is the priestly architecture of divine continuity, where covenantal shadows yield to messianic substance, and the eternal priesthood stands unveiled. Hebrews 8:8-12

Ιδου ημεραι ερχονται λεγει Κυριος και συντελεσω επι τον οικον Ισραηλ και επι τον οικον Ιουδα διαθηκην καινην ου κατα την διαθηκην ην εποιησα τοις πατρασιν αυτων εν ημερα επιλαβομενου

μου της χειρος αυτων εξαγαγειν αυτους εκ γης Αιγυπτου οτι αυτοι
ουκ ενεμειναν εν τη διαθηκη μου καγω ημελησα αυτων λεγει
Κυριος οτι αυτη η διαθηκη ην διαθησομαι τω οικω Ισραηλ μετα τας
ημερας εκεινας λεγει Κυριος διδους νομους μου εις την διανοιαν
αυτων και επι καρδιας αυτων επιγραψω αυτους και εσομαι αυτοις
εις Θεον και αυτοι εσονται μοι εις λαον και ου μη διδαξωσιν
εκαστος τον πολιτην αυτου και εκαστος τον αδελφον αυτου λεγων
γνωθι τον Κυριον οτι παντες ειδησουσιν με απο μικρου εως
μεγαλου αυτων οτι ιλεως εσομαι ταις αδικιαις αυτων και των
αμαρτιων αυτων ου μη μνησθησομαι ετι

On the Continuity Between Prophecy and Fulfillment: A Reflection on Jeremiah 31 and Hebrews 8. The English for the above is as follows:

For in finding fault with the people, He says, "BEHOLD, DAYS ARE COMING, SAYS THE LORD, WHEN I WILL BRING ABOUT A NEW COVENANT
WITH THE HOUSE OF ISRAEL AND THE HOUSE OF JUDAH, NOT LIKE THE COVENANT WHICH I MADE WITH THEIR FATHERS ON THE DAY I TOOK THEM BY THE HAND TO BRING THEM OUT OF THE LAND OF EGYPT; FOR THEY DID NOT CONTINUE IN MY COVENANT, AND I DID NOT CARE ABOUT THEM, SAYS THE LORD. "FOR THIS IS THE COVENANT WHICH I WILL MAKE WITH THE HOUSE OF IS-RAEL AFTER THOSE DAYS, DECLARES THE LORD: I WILL PUT MY LAWS INTO THEIR MINDS, AND WRITE THEM ON THEIR HEARTS. AND I WILL BE THEIR GOD, AND THEY SHALL BE MY PEOPLE. - NASB20

Just what is the connection between a prophecy and its fulfillment? The obvious answer would be intent. Intent, in sacred literature, is not merely authorial, it is divine. And so the question deepens: Is there a consistency between Jeremiah 31 and Hebrews 8, that is not only in language but in covenantal purpose?

Hebrews 8 is not a neutral citation. It is a polemic, a deliberate theological maneuver. Its invocation of Jeremiah is not a passive remembrance it is an active application. The author of Hebrews seeks to establish content, and to redirect it. And so we must ask: What was Jeremiah's context? What was the prophetic burden under which he wrote?

Jeremiah 31 emerges from exile, from covenant rupture, from the ache of a people who had broken faith. It is not a prophecy of replacement, it is quite the opposite, it is one of restoration. "I will make a new covenant," says YHWH, not with a new people, with the house of Israel and the house of Judah. The continuity is ethnic, covenantal, and historical. The Torah is not discarded; it is internalized. The law is not abolished; it is written on the heart.

When Hebrews 8 cites this passage, the tone shifts. The covenant is still "new," but the referent is broadened, the context reoriented. The polemic of Hebrews leans toward discontinuity, toward a rupture that some theologians have mistaken for divine intent. But is this rupture real, or is it a misreading born of theological presupposition?

Translation, too, plays its part. One would suppose that a faithful translation would exhibit continuity, would preserve Jeremiah's context, his covenantal vision, his prophetic cadence. But this is not always the case. Translators, like theologians, are not immune to agenda. Have they intended, as the prophet did, to maintain purpose and continuity? Or have they, consciously or not, allowed theological bias to fracture the thread?

James D.G. Dunn recounts this problem well. James D. G. Dunn was a typographic irritant to the Reformation's monoculture, blessedly so. He refused to let "covenant" be reduced to shorthand into a forensic transaction or a Protestant slogan. Dunn's insistence on Second Temple Judaism as the interpretive backdrop for Paul exposed the semantic drift that had turned *berit* into a courtroom abstraction.

He reminded us that covenant is not a contract but a communal architecture, relational, participatory, and deeply Jewish. His work on the "New Perspective on Paul" didn't just tweak Pauline theology; it reintroduced covenant as a living scaffold, not a dead ledger. Dunn's legacy is restorationist in the best sense: he re-inked the glyphs that had faded under centuries of theological shorthand. He notes the dispute among theologians over the continuity of Scripture, and rightly so. He says:

> *"One of the major issues which has resurfaced in current discussions of Pauline theology is the question of his gospel's newness. Was Paul's gospel in the last analyst simply a re-expression of God's centuries old summons to Israel? Or did it constitute a decisive break with everything that had gone before? The first question suggests what might be called a heilsgeschichtlich perspective, where the emphasis is on the line of continuity from Abraham, through Moses, David and the prophets, climaxing in Jesus, and on to Paul"* [1]

The tension is not academic, it is sacred. If the New Covenant is indeed the fulfillment of Jeremiah's vision, then it must honor the original context. It must preserve the covenantal integrity of Israel, not erase it. This is not a call for nostalgia, nor a romanticized of the past, nor is it for rigid literalism. It is a call for reverence, for a hermeneutic that listens before it speaks, that preserves before it re-purposes. The manuscript speaks, yes, when we allow it to speak in its own voice, not ours. What James D.G. Dunn rightly points to is not merely a hermeneutical tension, it is a schism in perspective, a divide between Judaism and Christianity that finds its sharpest edge in the interpretation of Paul. The issue is not just Paul's gospel, it is Shaul's relationship to the Tenach. For all the technical rumination, the endless parsing of Greek participles and covenantal clauses, one thing is rarely considered: the destructive potential of misunderstanding Shaul. II Peter 3:16 remains disturbingly relevant. "There are some things in [Shaul's letters] hard to understand," Peter writes, "which the ignorant and unstable twist to their own destruction." The warning is not about Shaul's clarity, but about the consequences of distortion. And distortion, in this case, has become institutionalized. It is not fringe, it is consensus. Did Shaul (Paul) and Jeremiah share a covenantal understanding? The question itself is often dismissed as naïve, or worse, heretical. It seems inconceivable to many theologians that Paul and Jeremiah are not antagonists. The presumption is rupture. The possibility that Paul, as he himself claims, was a "minister of the New Covenant" in harmony with Jeremiah is, for many, beyond the pale. It is not even considered. And yet, the author of Hebrews cites Jeremiah. Scholars cite Jeremiah. But few dare to challenge the consensus that pits Shaul against the prophets. Instead, they construct elaborate theological epicycles, layer upon layer of deferents, eccentrics, and equants, reminiscent of pre-Copernican astronomy. The goal is not clarity, but preservation of a system. Shaul's hermeneutics are overlaid with artificial constructs to maintain a modern theological model, even when that model contradicts the textual witness. Shaul's hermeneutics were not born in abstraction. They were forged in Jerusalem, shaped by revelation, and clarified in Arabia. 2 Corinthians 3:6 is not a geographical footnote, it is a theological declaration. Paul did not go up to Jerusalem to receive instruction. He went into Arabia, into the wilderness, into the place of covenantal encounter. Like Moses. Like Elijah. Like Jeremiah. He said something quite troubling, He said:

ημας διακονους καινης διαθηκης - II Corinthians 3:6 [2]
English: we are servants of the new covenant

This is doubly troubling when Shaul says, "I did not receive it from man, nor was I taught it, I received it through a revelation of Yeshua the Messiah." The gospel he preached was not a break with the Tenach, but its unveiling. The covenant was not discarded, it was fulfilled. The Torah was not abolished, it was internalized.

And yet, the consensus persists. The 'push back' is reinforced. There is often a theological doubling down this error. The manuscript speaks, but its voice is muffled beneath layers of theological sediment. The task, then, is not to innovate, but to excavate. To recover the voice of Shaul, not as a founder of a new religion, but as a witness to the covenant renewed.

By declaring, "I am a minister of a new covenant" (2 Corinthians 3:6), Shaul does more than assert apostolic authority he invokes a seismic shift in covenantal consciousness. The issue becomes the Greek syntax, which lacks the definite article. καινης διαθηκης Not της καινης διαθηκης. Not "the" new covenant. Does this grammatical subtlety sever the thread that ties Shaul to Jeremiah's prophecy? Does the absence of definition become the theological scalpel that carves the blank white page between what is now call the "Old Testament" and the "New Testament"?

Translation and the Fracturing of Prophetic Continuity

Should we, by the same logic, speak of *an* old covenant? *An* old testament? The absurdity reveals itself. The phrase "Old Testament" is not a textual designation, it is a theological imposition. It presumes rupture. It presumes replacement. But Jeremiah did not speak of a discarded covenant. He spoke of a renewed one. A covenant written not on stone, but on hearts. If the Mount of Transfiguration [3] were a post-Apostolic invention, it would read like a rabbinic disputation. Yeshua, Moshe, and Eliyahu locked in soteriological debate, parsing the nature of covenantal continuity. Instead, we are given a scene of convergence. No dispute. No rupture. Only glory. The Law, the Prophets, and the Messiah in luminous harmony. Yet, modern theology often renders Shaul and the disciples as glorified *sommeliers*, pouring the "new wine" of Luke 22:20 with little understanding of its vintage. The implication is uncouth. It reduces covenantal theology to ecclesial service. But Shaul was no waiter. He was a witness. A minister. A διακονος of the covenant Jeremiah foresaw.

We need to be clear: a *new covenant* is not the same as a *New Testament*. The former is relational, prophetic, eschatological. The latter is editorial, ecclesial, and often misleading. Charles Ryrie, in his dispensational framework, makes this distinction explicit. He writes:

> "Therefore, the material of the Old Testament is distinguished from that of the New." [4]

Further more he goes on to write:

> "There is no interpreter of the Bible who does not recognize the need for certain basic distinction in the Scriptures. The theological liberal, no mater how much he speaks of the Judaistic background of Christianity, recognizes that Christiainity is nevertheless different from Judaism" [5]

What this does indicate, beneath the surface of theological posturing, is that the cause of such recognition is not textual fidelity, but self-perception. Projection. One's theological conclusions are often determined not by exegesis, but by one's identity. Who you are, how you locate yourself within the sacred narrative, is determinative for these recognitions. The interpreter does not merely read the text; he reads himself into it.

Epicycles, Ontologies, and the Ecclesial Machinery

In this case, he may be putting words into the mouth of his opponents, namely, Covenant Theology, though I would suspect they would not object to the differentiations he draws. They might even welcome them, so long as the categories remain intact. He does mention Judaism, though not to engage its impute in the discussion. He considers it wholly other, a school of thought entirely separate, not merely in doctrine but in ontology. Judaism, for its part, is fine with this. It has long desired to be left alone, to be unentangled from the ecclesial machinery of Christendom.

It is apparent that he sees Dispensationalism and Covenant Theology not as variations within a shared framework, but as different kinds. Is this truly the case? From the outside, they appear more as differences in degree, two systems orbiting the same theological center, each with its own epicycles and deferents.

Another school of thought declines to revolve around that axis. That being a Messianic perspective. This is not a system imposed from above, but a posture derived from within. From those who are, as Paul writes in Ephesians 2:12, "included in the commonwealth of Israel." It is a perspective born of grafting, of being brought near, of being declared either "wild branches" (Gentiles) or "natural branches" (Israel), both of whom constitute the body.

Christendom's theological architecture must hold these expressions to be inverted. The Gentiles must become the 'natural branches'. The Israelis must become the wild ones. The commonwealth of Israel must be deleted, and the Church inserted in its place. The grafting must be reversed. The nearness must be redefined. And in doing so, the theological operation begins to resemble not covenantal inclusion, but surgical erasure, epispasm and infibulation, both physical and spiritual.

There is a theological and hermeneutical position outside these frameworks, one that is devoid of supersessionism. Whether punitive, economic, or structural, it matters not. The text declares: *Romans 11:2, God hath not cast away His people.* The Olive Tree remains. The commonwealth of Israel has not been superceded. The New Covenant is not cut with the Church. It is cut with the House of Israel and the House of Judah.

Who here can imagine the prophet Jeremiah as a supersessionist? Who can envision him proclaiming a covenant that erases the very people to whom it was promised? Skipping over, for now, the glaring omission, the lack of recognition that biblical Judaism and rabbinic Judaism have long since diverged, particularly over the role and mechanism of atoning, that is addressed in the second book in this series, we shall move on. The fracture is not merely historical; it is theological, or you might say 'interpretive'. But for the sake of the present argument, we will bracket that distinction and proceed. This is the theological hedge. The attempt to preserve Israel's covenant while granting the Church its benefits. But if Paul is a minister of that covenant, then the Church is not merely a participant, it is a grafted-in possessor. The article may be absent, but the context is unmistakable. The manuscript speaks. The covenant endures. The notion of fracture is a construct. This brings us to the next proposition of Ryrie, where he writes: *"Any person is a dispensationalist who trusts in the blood of Christ rather than bringing an animal sacrifice."* [6] This is missing the point. We are that point. You are that point, not the animals. As Rabbi Gary Beresford rightly observed, *"The Messiah did not die for the animals. He died for us."* [7] He did not come to spare bulls and goats from the altar. The role the animals functioned as should be seen as intrinsically linked to the Messiah's kafar. Animal sacrifice is the blood-ink echo of Yeshua's kafar; they cannot be unbound without semantic collapse. This is how they are to be discerned, this is their purpose, they stand as a witness. His atoning work is ours. It is personal, covenantal, and transformative. But it is not, as some suppose, the termination of animal sacrifices. The validity of the sacrificial system lies in two things. First, it is prophetic. It points forward. It anticipates. This is not speculation, it is Scripture. Ezekiel chapters 40 through 48 lay out a vision of restored Temple worship, complete with offerings. The future Temple in Ezekiel could be a testimony that all that had happened was for a purpose, it is the restoration of that witness found in the narative of chapters 40 - 48. Not abolished. Not spiritualized. Restored to their status as witness to Messiah's kafar. He is and will be 'kafar' to us. We must not view what happened as a failure in part of God's plan but a functioning part of the whole of God's intent. The idea that what occured in the 'Old Testament' was a failed exercise is a tragic notion. The LORD did not proclaim He was starting a new religion two millenium ago. There is only one plan. We should be living by every word. All God's word must be seen as a whole, not as two competing testaments.

Second, Yeshua's disciples continued offering sacrifice.[8] They did not see His death as a negation of the altar, but as its fulfillment. Fulfillment is the convergence of meaning and manifestation. They went to the Temple as recorded in Acts 2:46; 3:1; 5:42.. They participated. They did not presume that the cross had rendered the altar obsolete. So the questions remain: Why did we make animal sacrifices? Why will we make them again? This is to establish that, the reality of the heavenly altar is eternal. God has not redecorated the heavenly tabernacle. That would be an alteration of the pattern. God did not commission Gian Lorenzo Bernini (1598–1680) to remodel the heavenly apse. The ultimate question would be, and may never be answered. It would be Why?

But perhaps the more pressing question is: Why aren't we making sacrifices now?

The answer is not theological innovation. It is obedience. Torah limits sacrifices to location and time. They are not to be made anywhere, at any time. They are not to be made on your backyard grill. Barbaque sauce and blood are not the same. They are not to be improvised or reimagined. Obedience to Torah precludes this. It is not the absence of sacrifice, it is the suspension of location. The altar is not gone. It is waiting.

To permit sacrifices outside of Torah would require a suspension of Torah itself. And once Torah is suspended, anything goes. You could swing a chicken over your head and call it atonement. But that is not obedience. That is parody.

The issue is not sacrifice. The issue is authority. And the authority is Torah.

The New Covenant, as declared in Hebrews 8:10, is not a new ethic. It is the same Torah, written on hearts and minds. Hebrews 8:10 says the exact same thing as Jeremiah 31:33, verbatim. There is no rupture. There is no replacement. There is only fulfillment.

We, as Gentiles, have not replaced Israel. We have joined her. There is but one new man. One body. One covenantal people. Avraham is father to us all, not by replacement, but by grafting. Not by erasure, by inclusion.

Issues. What are the issues? What needs to be addressed next?

Is *a* New Covenant being spoken of, or *the* New Covenant? Is it singular or plural? Is a covenant *cut* or *made*? What is a covenant? What is a testament?

These are not idle questions. They are structural. They determine how we read, how we teach, how we live. The problem with the "New Covenant" is not its existence, it is how it is understood.

The New Covenant of Hebrews 8:7–12 is not a future hope. It is a present reality. It is a statement about what *is*. Not what will be. Not what might be. What *is*.

This leads us to the issue of ratification. In Hebrews 8:6, the Greek word νενομοθέτηται, translated "was established", is not incidental. It is a reference to prior ratification. The covenant is not awaiting validation. It has already been validated. The grammar is not speculative. It is declarative.

And this statement is not isolated. It is embedded within a sustained narrative concerning the High Priest. Hebrews 6:19 through 11:31 is a theological arc every verse reinforcing the nature of priesthood and the role of the High Priest.

The mediation of the High Priest within the New Covenant is the point. That is what Hebrews 8:1 *is saying*. Not implying. Not suggesting. *Is saying*.

The covenant is not theoretical. It is priestly. It is active. It is mediated.

We must return to the foundational questions:

- Is the New Covenant singular or plural?
- Is it cut or made?
- What is a covenant?
- What is a testament?

These four are not academic exercises. They are exegetical imperatives. They shape our theology, our obedience, our continuity with Israel.

The New Covenant is not a theological abstraction. It is textual. It is rooted. It is named.

It is found in Jeremiah 31:31, or in the Septuagint, Jeremiah 38:31. It is echoed in Matthew 26:28, Luke 22:20, 2 Corinthians 3:6, Hebrews 8:8, 8:13, 9:15, and 12:24. The ratification is recounted in 1 Corinthians 11:25, which itself references Mark 14:24. These are not scattered fragments, they are a liturgical thread. A covenantal tapestry.

This brings us to the next major topic: What is the nature of a covenant?

Covenants were common in the ancient Near East, particularly during the Late Bronze Age (15th to 13th centuries B.C.E.). We possess a wealth of extant manuscripts from across the Fertile Crescent, Hittite treaties, Assyrian suzerainty contracts, and Egyptian diplomatic texts. These are not incidental. They are context. It is always necessary to look at the setting of the Late Bronze Age. But this is a two-edged sword.

On one edge: Did the social and political thought of the ANE form the origin of the biblical covenant? Was Israel merely adapting the diplomatic norms of its neighbors?

On the other edge: Do the parallels among these ancient cultures demonstrate that they intersect with biblical covenant, not merely run alongside it?

It is clear that the majority of scholarship is persuaded that this is the case. That the biblical covenant is not sui generis, that is unique in its category, but emerges from a shared cultural matrix. That the form, preamble, stipulations, blessings, curses, witnesses, is not unique to Sinai, but echoes the treaty structures of the ANE.

But the question remains: Is the biblical covenant merely parallel, or is it polemical? Is it borrowing, or is it subverting?

The covenant of YHWH is not a contract. It is not a negotiation. It is a declaration. It is cut, not signed. It is ratified in blood, not ink. It is relational, not transactional.

So yes, the ANE treaties provide a framework. But the biblical covenant provides a rupture. It is not merely ancient, it is eternal.

The New Covenant is not a theological abstraction, it is a textual reality. It is found in Jeremiah 31:31 (LXX Jeremiah 38:31), Matthew 26:28, Luke 22:20, 2 Corinthians 3:6, Hebrews 8:8, 8:13, 9:15, and 12:24. Its ratification is recounted in 1 Corinthians 11:25, which itself references Mark 14:24. These are not scattered echoes. The covenant is not merely promised, it is enacted.

Blueprints of Mercy: Covenant as Sacred Architecture in a World of Treaties

This brings us to the next major topic: What is the nature of a covenant?

Covenants were common in the Ancient Near East, particularly in the Late Bronze Age (15th to 13th centuries B.C.E.). We possess a wealth of extant manuscripts across the Fertile Crescent, Hittite suzerainty treaties, Babylonian contracts, Assyrian loyalty oaths. The setting matters. But it is a two-edged sword.

On one edge: Did the social and political thought of the ANE form the origin of the biblical covenant? On the other: Do the parallels among these ancient cultures demonstrate that they intersect with biblical covenant, not merely run alongside it?

Joshua A. Berman has brought this out clearly. Joshua A. Berman, of Bar-Ilan University, is a biblical scholar and Orthodox rabbi whose work on covenant theology and ancient Near Eastern treaty structures makes him a vital voice in any restorationist discussion of of architecture and meaning. He writes:

> *"What is the original, biblical meaning of covenant? As some scholars first noted fifty years ago, the pact between God and Israel bears a strong resemblance to the ANE suzerainty treaty between a sovereign king and a subordinate king."*

This leads us to the first historical issue: the parallels of said suzerainty treaties in the ANE. George E. Mendenhall's seminal colloquium, *Law and Covenant in Israel and the Ancient Near East*, is indispensable here. George E. Mendenhall was a pioneering biblical scholar whose work on ancient Near Eastern treaty forms reshaped how scholars understand covenant in the Hebrew Bible. I would point you to Part II, where he offers a detailed comparison of Hittite treaty structures and biblical covenant forms.

There are flaws. The structure of biblical covenants stems not from diplomatic convention, but from the nature of relationship between the parties—and more importantly, from the origin and authorship of the covenant itself. Mendenhall himself notes:

> *"Similarly, the Hittite language, and the Babylonian as well, never had a single word for contract or covenant. In both languages the covenant was designated by a phrase which would be translated literally as 'oath and bonds.'"* [9]

This is a textually demonstrative problem for parallelism. If there is no single word, then there is no true cognate. Parallels demand a linguistic anchor. And here, the anchor fails.

Does בְּרִית (brit, covenant) have a cognate in Hattic, Akkadian, Urartan, Hurrian, Sumerian, or Hittite? The answer is no. Translating these terms into English, pact, treaty, covenant, contract, agreement, league, only exposes the semantic flaw. Hebrew has one word, not many. *Brit* is the word. The only word at issue. Its use in the biblical corpus has no synonyms. No substitutes. No semantic dilution.

And as for structure, consider the sign/seal of a בְּרִית. The rarity of an analogous sign in ANE treaties is striking. The sign of the Avrahamic covenant, and its codification in the Mosaic covenant, is the product of כָּרַת, cutting. Circumcision. A physical mark. A covenantal incision. Not a signature. Not a stamp. A wound. This is not diplomacy. This is devotion.

One appellation *treaty* may be subdivided into two distinct forms: (a) suzerainty and (b) parity. This classification, first systematized by Dr. Viktor Korosec in his 1931 publication [10], is not merely academic. Dr. Viktor Korosec was a Yugoslav legal historian whose 1931 analysis of Hittite treaty structures laid the groundwork for modern biblical covenant studies. It implies a caste relationship. The provisions of such treaties presuppose not just political hierarchy, but ontological stratification. This is no minor footnote—it is a fissure in the foundation. The issue of class delineation within covenantal frameworks must be addressed at length elsewhere, for it touches the very nerve of divine authorship and human reception.

Yet one further analogous problem arises, as rightly noted by Joshua Berman of Bar-Ilan University in his work *Who Was the Vassal King of the Sinai Covenant?* He writes:

> "*Yet who is it within these covenantal passages that stands parallel to the vassal king? In the Pentateuch it is true that Israel has a leader: Moses. Yet, Moses may not be properly termed a king. He is never referred to through this term: his children are not his heirs.*" [11]

This is not a semantic oversight, it is a structural anomaly. If the Sinai covenant is to be read through the lens of ANE suzerainty, then where is the vassal king? Moses, though central, is not dynastic. He is not enthroned. His authority is charismatic, not hereditary. His sons do not inherit his office. The absence of succession is the absence of sovereignty.

You could just as easily insert feudal inferences into this matrix as suzerain ones. The status of the subordinate is open to question. For in the biblical corpus, God, the suzerain, is not delegating rule to a human king. He is establishing direct governance over His nation. There is no throne beneath the throne. And it will be a considerable time before a king is introduced at all.

Indeed, the introduction of a human king, namely Shaul, violated the covenantal architecture. But the Sinai covenant was broken long before Shaul's coronation. And it was not broken by the appointment of a representative. It was broken by the rejection of God Himself as king.

This rupture is recorded in *1 Samuel 8:5–20*. The people demand a king, not to fulfill a covenant, but to replace it. They do not reject Moses. They reject God. The text is unambiguous:

> *"It is not you they have rejected, but they have rejected me as their king."* (v.7) *"We want a king over us. Then we will be like all the other nations."* (vv.19–20)

This is not a request for representation. It is a theological mutiny. The people are not seeking a vassal, they are seeking a buffer. They want a subordinate to stand between them and the divine. They want to be like the nations. But Israel was never meant to be like the nations. The covenant was not a treaty, it was a divine adoption. To demand a king was to reject sonship. To reject sonship was to reject God.

I am not denying the existence of parallels. That would be both historically naïve and textually dishonest. Parallels exist. They are real. They are instructive. Tim Hegg, in his work *The Covenant of Grant and the Abrahamic Covenant*, has detailed these with precision. His analysis rightly draws attention to the structural and linguistic affinities between Ancient Near Eastern grant covenants and the biblical Abrahamic covenant.

I would suggest that the value of these parallels lies not in proving derivation, but in establishing parameters. They help us understand the relational framework between Israel and her neighbors. They provide diplomatic context. More importantly, they illuminate the conditions of the theocracy, the divine governance of Israel. The covenant is not merely a treaty. It is not merely a grant. It is a declaration of divine rule. The parallels may help us understand the form, but they cannot account for the source. The biblical covenant is not a cultural artifact, it is a theological rupture. It is sui generis, a Latin phrase meaning "of its own kind" or "unique in its category." . It is cut, not copied.

It is here we need to look at the first of the texts to which I previously cited, and we must do so in chronological order. This is not a mere academic exercise, it is necessary to reconstruct the current state of affairs, so we understand how and why we are where we are. Theology without chronology is abstraction. We should always start at the beginning.

The context having been established, the covenantal fracture, the exile, the longing for restoration, we now turn to the prophetic word given to Jeremiah. Namely, the prophecy in Chapter 31. Beginning in verse 31 and running to verse 34 (LXX 38:31–34), we encounter not just a promise, but a rupture in covenantal expectation:

> "Behold, the days are coming," declares the Lord, "when I will make a new covenant with the house of Israel and the house of Judah , - not like the covenant that I made with their fathers on the day when I took them by the hand to bring them out of the land of Egypt, my covenant that they broke, though I was their husband," declares the Lord. "But this is the covenant that I will make with the house of Israel after those days," declares the Lord: "I will put my law within them, and I will write it on their hearts. And I will be their God, and they shall be my people. And no longer shall each one teach his neighbor and each his brother, saying, 'Know the Lord,' for

they shall all know me, from the least of them to the greatest," declares the Lord. "For I will forgive their iniquity, and I will remember their sin no more."

The following chronological review is not a mere survey of events. It is primarily designed to focus on two words, two anchors of covenantal theology, and their morphology and syntax. **These words are not incidental. They are foundational.**

The first is בְּרִית (*brit*), phonetically rendered as "breet," translated into English as *covenant*. The second is כָּרַת (*karath*), meaning *to cut*. These two will be referenced consistently throughout, and for ease of cross-reference, they will be color-coded in the manuscript overlays.

Why these two? Because in Hebrew, one does not "make" a covenant. One *cuts* it. The phrase is כָּרַת בְּרִית (*karath brit*)—to cut a covenant. This is not metaphor. It is visceral. It evokes blood, sacrifice, and solemnity. The morphology of כָּרַת spans Qal perfects, imperfects, imperatives, and participles, each carrying weight depending on context, whether the covenant is being initiated, recalled, or broken.

בְּרִית, meanwhile, is not a contract. It is a sacred bond. It appears in Genesis 15, where God alone walks the covenant path. It appears in Exodus, where blood seals the national calling. And it appears in Jeremiah 31, where the covenant is no longer external, it is inscribed upon the heart.

This review will trace the chronological unfolding of these terms, beginning with Genesis and culminating in the prophetic vision of Jeremiah. Only by following their linguistic and theological trajectory can we reconstruct the current state of affairs, and understand how and why we are where we are.

It is here where the Westminster Leningrad Codex [4.14] below serves as the representative of the originals for my treatment of Jeremiah's covenant proclamation. I am not appealing to abstraction or theological synthesis, I am grounding this in the received text.

The passage in question is Jeremiah 31:33, which in the Hebrew reads:

כִּי זֹאת הַבְּרִית אֲשֶׁר אֶכְרֹת אֶת־בֵּית יִשְׂרָאֵל אַחֲרֵי הַיָּמִים הָהֵם נְאֻם־יְהוָה נָתַתִּי אֶת־תּוֹרָתִי בְּקִרְבָּם וְעַל־לִבָּם אֶכְתֲּבֶנָּה וְהָיִיתִי לָהֶם לֵאלֹהִים וְהֵמָּה יִהְיוּ־לִי לְעָם

The English translation: Because this the covenant that I will cut with the house of Israel; After those days, saith the LORD, I will put my law in their inward parts, and write it in their hearts; and will be their God, and they shall be my people.

This is not a generic promise. It is a covenantal incision. The word בְּרִית (brit), covenant, appears here with deliberate force, and is qualified by כָּרַת (karath), to cut. These two terms will be color-coded throughout the manuscript for ease of cross-reference, as they form the linguistic and theological spine of this study.

Note the syntax: נתתי את תורתי בקרבם ועל לבם אכתבנה - "I will give my Torah within them, and upon their hearts I will write it." This is not a new ethic. It is a renewed inscription. The Torah is not abolished, it is internalized. The covenant is not replaced, it is re-cut.

This verse is the hinge. It is where prophetic promise meets covenantal continuity. And it is where our reconstruction must begin. The use of the term בְּרִית (brit) carries no ontological or class stratification limits. It is not reserved for kings, priests, or elites. It is not confined to divine-human interaction. The sole qualifier in the text is whether or not it is כָּרַת cut. That is the threshold. That is the criterion. If it is cut, it is covenant.

Its uses are as follows:

a. Person to person b. Person to group c. God to person d. God to nation e. Nation to nation f. Scroll g. Furniture

Yes, furniture. The covenantal scope is not limited to moral agents. It extends to objects, to artifacts, to the physical symbols of divine encounter. The Ark of the Covenant is not metaphor, it is material. The scroll of the covenant is not allegory, it is inscribed.

This breadth of usage dismantles any attempt to impose caste or class onto the term. The covenant is not stratified, it is sanctified. Its authority is not derived from the status of the parties, but from the act of cutting.

Time to Cut to the chase.

I wish to point out the obvious: the morphology, syntax, and phonology of בְּרִית (brit) are Hebrew. Not Hittite. Not Akkadian. Not Sumerian. Hebrew. The word that qualifies it כָּרַת (karath, to cut) is also Hebrew, and its meaning is contextually driven. Hebrew is contextually driven. This makes בְּרִית inseparable from כָּרַת, not merely by grammar, but by subject matter. The covenant is not made, it is cut. And that cutting is not metaphorical, it is sacrificial.

It is here where בְּרִית diverges from any parallels in the Ancient Near East. Dr. Viktor Korosec was a Yugoslav legal historian whose 1931 analysis of Hittite treaty structures laid the groundwork for modern biblical covenant studies. Dr. Viktor Korosec (1899–1985), in his 1931 analysis [12] of Hittite law and treaty forms, offers a six-part structure for suzerainty treaties:

1. **Preamble** – Identification of the sovereign
2. **Historical Prologue** – Recounting past relations
3. **Stipulations** – Obligations of the vassal
4. **Provisions for Deposit and Public Reading**
5. **List of Witnessing Deities**
6. **Curses and Blessings (Formulas)**

This structure is insightful, but it does not apply to the seven distinct uses of בְּרִית within the biblical corpus. Korosec's extensive knowledge of Hittite law is not in question. What is in question is its relevance to the authorship of the **Tanakh**. The biblical covenant is not a diplomatic document, it is a divine declaration. It is not witnessed by gods, it is authored by **YHWH**. It is not deposited in sanc-tuaries—it is inscribed on hearts.

The biblical covenant does not conform to ANE treaty architec-ture. It transcends it. It is not parity. It is not suzerainty. It is theoc-racy.

The fifth point is not decorative, it's the structural hinge. It bears the semantic weight of the covenant's structure and exposes the frac-ture most in need of exposition. . There is no other god in the Tanakh. The use of elohim in the plural is another topic, a topic best dealt with be Dr Heiser, Dr. Michael S. Heiser was an American biblical scholar best known for his work on the unseen realm, divine council theology, and ancient Semitic texts. This is not the moment to open a debate on the plural form *Elohim,* perhaps in another volume, where the ten-sion between grammatical plurality and theological singularity can be properly dissected. But suffice it to say: there is only one HaShem.

The deity was not a witness to this covenant. The witnesses, as explicitly stated, were the heavens and the earth. The deity was the principal party, not a bystander. This distinction is not semantic, it is structural. And it is precisely here that two imposed errors arise. First, the aforementioned suzerain parallelism, which attempts to retrofit biblical covenant into ANE treaty frameworks. Second, the use of the-ological eisegesis as a hermeneutic—a method that imports foreign categories into sacred text under the guise of interpretation.

It is dangerous, structurally dangerous, when scholars ignore the semantic pressure that a target language exerts upon the source lan-guage's hermeneutics. This is not a passive drift; it's a tectonic shift. Translation is not a neutral act. It is a theological act, a covenantal rendering. And how one guards the context from a calque, a calque be-ing a word or phrase borrowed from another language by literal trans-lation, often smuggling foreign syntax or meaning into native soil, whether linguistic or cultural, is not optional. It is essential. This is especially perilous in translation work, where the failure to acknowl-edge that concepts are autochthonous, that is, native to their own land, born of their own historical soil, not transplanted from foreign syntax or cultural pots, should be conspicuous. To miss this is to misread the scaffold and rebind the text with foreign ligatures.

One particularly egregious example is the word church. If there were any consensus within Christendom, it would be that the etymological context must be omitted. But omission is not fidelity, it is erasure. I speak here of Ephesians 2:11–13, which is definitive for the constituent parts and the use of the Hebrew words קָהָל (qahal) and עֵדָה (edah) [13] . These are not ecclesiastical abstractions, they are covenantal designations. They refer to the gathered assembly and the witnessing congregation. They are not interchangeable with *ekklesia* as later defined by Greco-Roman or Germanic ecclesiology. This is blatantly rendered by both the KJV (1611) and the ASV (1901) as in Acts 7:38. What a vision, as Brother Silas stood atop a rock, clutching a scroll and a tambourine. "Welcome, saints," he bellowed, "to First Sinai Church of the Wilderness. We're gathered here today under the leadership of Pastor Moses, who's fresh off a forty-day fast and still glowing from his mountaintop retreat."

The irony here is thick. Greek and Germanic understandings are considered legitimate calques, while biblical connections via the LXX are deemed "not kosher" [sic]. The same criticism applies to the so-called *messianic movement*, which itself suffers from a lack of consensus. The recent doctrinal reversal by FFOZ is symptomatic of this instability. For the community, it is the intrinsic constituting principle that matters. There is no separation between the Lord and His word. To sever the two is to dismantle the covenant.

Yeshua said:

ο δε απεκριθη ειπεν· γεγραπται οτι ουκ επ' αρτω μονω ζησεται ο ανθρωπος αλλ' επι παντι ρηματι εκπορευομενω δια στοματος θεου

(*But He answered and said, "It is written: Man shall not live by bread alone, but by every word that proceeds from the mouth of God."*)

The **γεγραπται** *it is written,* is not a mere citation. It is His authority. It is His Word, written in the **Torah**. This is not a proof-text, it is a declaration of covenantal continuity. The phrase כַּכָּתוּב in Hebrew, "as it is written," occurs in this exact form some 80 times throughout the Tanakh. But the point here is not statistical, it is theological.

The point is Devarim (Deuteronomy) 8:3:

> *"And He humbled you and let you hunger, and fed you with manna, which you did not know, nor did your fathers know, that He might make you understand that man does not live by bread alone, but man lives by every word that comes from the mouth of the LORD."*

So far, we have reviewed the academic aspects of covenant, its structure, its legal contours, its historical echoes. But now I must correct a potential problem, one that is not merely semantic but seismic.

A relationship with the God of Avraham, Yitzḥak, and Ya'akov is not casual, not conceptual, it is covenantal. It is not a feeling, not a philosophy, it is status. And if one is not in the New Covenant, one has no relationship with the Creator. That is not exclusionary rhetoric, it is theological reality.

What I am proposing is not novel. It is precisely what Jeremiah wrote:

> *"Behold, days are coming,"* declares the LORD, *"when I will cut a new covenant..."* This covenant is not external, it is innate. It is not written on tablets of stone, but on the tablets of the heart. It is not mediated by institution, but by indwelling.

This is not a rhetorical exercise. This is a shift from theological tourism, where one visits sacred concepts like museum exhibits to covenantal citizenship, where one lives inside the scaffold, bound by its ligatures and sustained by its altar stones. This is a paradigm

shift. The New Covenant is not a theological upgrade, it is the only valid passport into relationship with the God of Israel. And if that sounds polemical, it is because the stakes are eternal.

Our Lord said something which no rabbi could object to:

> *"Man shall live by every word."* This includes the portion quoted from the Torah. It is not selective. It is not partial. It is every word. The γεγραπται - "it is written" - is not a rhetorical flourish. It is a declaration of authority. It is the Word of HaShem, inscribed in the Torah, and binding upon the believer.

What I hope to show is tantamount to a paradigm shift in theology. That the Lord meant what He said. That all of His Word is to be lived by. Not admired. Not allegorized. Lived. Theology and hermeneutics ought to reflect this declaration. Not just in theory, but in operation. A theological position that recognizes the entirety of the Word and makes it functional, embodied, enacted, obeyed.

So the question must be asked: Has this been the case?

During the Second Temple period, the role of the prophet was not merely to proclaim, it was to exegete. Prophetic authority was textual. Could Jeremiah have envisioned a Torah devoid of content? A covenant without commandments? A Word without weight?

What criteria did Jeremiah employ?

I would propose that Isaiah 40:8 and Psalm 119:152 are essential to our understanding:

יָבֵשׁ חָצִיר נָבֵל צִיץ וּדְבַר אֱלֹהֵינוּ יָקוּם לְעוֹלָם קֶדֶם יָדַעְתִּי מֵעֵדוֹתֶיךָ כִּי לְעוֹלָם יְסַדְתָּם

> *"The grass withers, the flower fades, but the word of our God stands forever."* (Isaiah 40:8) *"Long ago I learned from your statutes that you established them to last forever."* (Psalm 119:152)

These are not poetic sentiments. They are theological axioms. The Word is eternal. The statutes are enduring. The covenant is not a temporary arrangement, it is a permanent inscription.

This is not a call to nostalgia. It is a call to return. To return to the Word that was spoken, written, and never revoked. To live by every word, not just the ones that fit our systems.

Were Jeremiah's four uses of "new" as an adjective for the covenant an indicator that there would be a content shift? That is the question. But it is not merely a lexical inquiry, it is a theological fault line. Does the nature of a salvific covenant allow for the abrogation of the eternal Torah by the medium of prophecy?

Let us be clear: Jeremiah was not issuing a policy statement. He was delivering a prophetic proclamation. And prophecy, by its nature, does not negate Torah, it reaffirms it. So we must ask: does a policy statement require a mediator? And if so, who mediates the abrogation of Sinai?

Just how could a change in Torah negate the Tabernacle in Heaven? Is the heavenly pattern, shown to Moshe on the mountain, now obsolete? Has the eternal been overwritten by the temporal?

Was Jeremiah, in declaring the New Covenant, violating Deuteronomy 13:1–5, the warning against prophets who lead the people away from the commandments? Was he suggesting that the people would no longer honor Exodus 19:9, where HaShem says:

וַיֹּאמֶר יְהוָה אֶל־מֹשֶׁה הִנֵּה אָנֹכִי בָּא אֵלֶיךָ בְּעַב הֶעָנָן בַּעֲבוּר יִשְׁמַע הָעָם בְּדַבְּרִי עִמָּךְ וְגַם־בְּךָ יַאֲמִינוּ לְעוֹלָם

"Behold, I will come to you in a thick cloud, so that the people may hear when I speak with you and may also believe in you forever."

Would Jeremiah dare to envision a Torah devoid of content? A covenant without commandments? A relationship without revelation?

I propose that he did not. I propose that Isaiah 40:8 and Psalm 119:152 are essential to our understanding:

"The grass withers, the flower fades, but the word of our God stands forever." "Long ago I learned from your statutes that you established them to last forever."

These are not poetic flourishes. They are theological anchors. The Word stands. The statutes endure. The covenant is not erased ,it is inscribed.

Jeremiah's use of "new" does not imply replacement. It implies renewal. The covenant is not annulled, it is internalized. The Torah is not discarded, it is written on hearts. And the Tabernacle in Heaven remains untouched, unshaken, and unnegotiable.

Would Jeremiah have sacrificed his prophetic authority in making such a pronouncement? The LORD had said that the children of Israel would hear Moshe forever. That is not a metaphor, it is a covenantal declaration. לְעוֹלָם is the term used. Eternal. Unrevoked. Immutable.

So we must ask: does the terminology Jeremiah employed indicate a Torah as proposed by Olufemi I. Adeyemi? [14] Olufemi I. Adeyemi is a biblical scholar known for his rigorous work on the New Covenant and the Law of Christ, particularly in relation to Jeremiah 31:33 and Pauline theology. His sourcing of the New Covenant is concise, yes, but to argue, as he does, for what is *possible* in defining what Torah is, is precarious. Possibility is not prophecy. Introducing eisegesis to redefine Torah under the banner of a "new covenant" will not suffice—not when the term לְעוֹלָם , for ever, as eternal as the author, proceeds from HaShem Himself.

The definite nature of this Torah has two grammatical considerations. First, it is the direct object of the LORD's action, as the use of אֶת clearly demands. Second, it is **not** written with the definite article. It is not אֶת־הַתּוֹרָתִי. To repeat: that is not how it is written. It is written as follows: אֶת־תּוֹרָתִי. The subject of the sentence—the one performing the action—is the LORD. This makes it unmistakably clear: this is His Torah.

Had the prophecy been that HaShem would be writing His Son's law on the heart and mind, somewhere He would have said so. But He did not. The eleven occurrences of *Torah* in Jeremiah, only three do not use the suffix to indicate that תּוֹרָתִי is genitive. The rest are explicit: it is His Torah.

So we return to the question: could Jeremiah have envisioned a Torah devoid of content? A covenant without commandments? A salvific shift that nullifies the eternal?

I propose that he did not. I propose that Deuteronomy 13:1–5 stands as a safeguard against such theological innovation. And I propose that Exodus 19:9, where HaShem declares that the people will hear Moshe *forever*, remains untouched.

To suggest otherwise is to sever the Word from the LORD. And that is a rupture no prophet would dare to make.

Now it is clear what this prophecy, and its fulfillment, is declaring about our relationship to the LORD.

It is not provisional. It is not symbolic. It is covenantal.

The Torah is not abolished, it is inscribed. The covenant is not re-placed, it is renewed. The relationship is not mediated by institution, it is direct, written on the heart and mind by the hand of HaShem Himself.

This is not theological speculation. It is prophetic reality. The New Covenant is not a rupture, it is a restoration. And our relationship to the LORD is not abstract, it is sealed in His Word.

Two

Translations from Wonderland

"Either the well was very deep, or she fell very slowly, for she had plenty of time as she went down to look about her and to wonder what was going to happen next." - Charles Lutwidge Dodgson 1865

The first of the translations was the LXX which calls into question the corpus of Greek Lexica. The LXX or known as the Septuagint from circa 132 BCE.

There are quite a number of Greek words that must be scrutinized. Their use in the Septuagint (LXX), and the trajectory they set for subsequent translations, is key to the misunderstanding of what eventually calcified into theology. Words are not neutral. They are vessels. And when mishandled, they become distortions. One does have to consider if this was motivated and/or intrepretive distortions? Let's not kid ourselves, words matter. The Greek ones are not an exception. There are several terms in the Septuagint (the ancient Greek translation of the Hebrew Scriptures) that need to be put under the microscope. Why? Because the way they were used shaped how theology was later misunderstood. It didn't start with doctrine, it started with diction.

Two words in particular: *diathēkē* (διαθηκη) and *diathēsomai* (διαθησομαι). The first is a noun, it means "covenant." The second is a verb, it means "I will covenant." They're linked like root and branch. I've marked *diathēkē* in brown and *diathēsomai* in orange in my overlays to show their theological weight.

Now here's the kicker: the translators had options. Four different Greek nouns they could've used for the Hebrew *berit*. They chose *diathēkē*. For the verb, they had five choices. They picked *diathēsomai*. That wasn't random. It was deliberate. They were shaping how the covenant would be understood through a Greek lens.

This is where the shift began. Not in councils. Not in creeds. In the words themselves.

The first two words under examination are διαθηκη and διαθησομαι. They are intrinsically linked. The first is a **noun**, the covenant itself. The second is a verb, the act of covenanting. I have assigned **brown** to represent διαθηκη and orange for διαθησομαι in the manuscript overlays. These colors are not arbitrary, they signal theological weight and grammatical function.

Phonically, διαθηκη is *Diathaykay*, and διαθησομαι is *Diathaysumai*. The distinction matters. One is the object, the other the action. One is the seal, the other the sealing.

It should be noted that the translators of that day had four lexical choices from which they selected διαθηκη. They also had five verbal options from which they chose διαθησομαι. This means they had a bent of nuance, a deliberate theological lens through which they rendered the Hebrew. They were not merely translating, they were interpreting. When it came to Jeremiah 38:31 the LXX rendered it:

Ιδου ημεραι ερχονται λεγει Κυριος και
διαθησομαι τω οικω Ισραηλ και τω οικω

The choice of *διαθηκη, meaning a disposition of property by will, not a covenant,* over alternatives like *συνθηκη* (agreement) or *ομολογια* (confession) signals a unilateral will, not a mutual contract. Likewise, the selection of *διαθησομαι, meaning to put apart or set aside,* over verbs like *συντιθημι* or *τιθημι* reveals a divine initiator, not a cutting.

This is where theology begins, not in the councils, but in the lexicon. And if we are to restore sacred meaning, we must begin with the words themselves.

What becomes clear upon reviewing the Greek lexica, specifically for *διαθηκην* (*diathēkēn*), is that there is a semantic problem in its use within the Greek-speaking world. It begs the question: what exactly was *Koine*? The lexicon itself draws a sharp demarcation between biblical and non-biblical usage. The question is not merely linguistic, it is theological. Why the divide?

Scott W. Hahn of Franciscan University, in Steubenville, Ohio, addresses this tension directly. In his critique [20] of *διαθηκη* as a translation for בְּרִית (*berit*), he outlines both the strengths and limitations of the term by breaking its usage into five analytical categories:

1. Legal Issues
2. Grammatical Issues
3. Lexical Issues
4. Syntactical Issues
5. Contextual Issues

Dr. Hahn rightly notes that as a translation, *διαθηκη* carries certain eventualities, semantic baggage that may not align with the Hebrew original. But I would emphasize this: context is king. The function of context, the original, source material, overrides lexical considerations in the target language. You cannot revise the source language to conform to the social institutions or conventions of the target language. That is not translation. That is theological colonization. So yes, *διαθηκη* carries semantic baggage. But the real issue isn't the suitcase, it's the itinerary. Where are we going with this term? What theological terrain are we crossing? And are we honoring the original map?

The translators of the Septuagint had four noun options for rendering בְּרִית, and they chose διαθηκη. For the verbal form, they had five choices, and selected διαθησομαι. This was not accidental. It was deliberate. They had a bent of nuance, a theological lens through which they shaped the understanding they wished to present.

This is where theology begins, not in the councils, but in the lexicon. And if we are to restore sacred meaning, we must begin with the words themselves.

The team of scholars who produced the Septuagint (LXX) had options, at least four Greek nouns at their disposal when translating the Hebrew בְּרִית (berit). But instead of choosing a term that preserved the covenantal gravity of Sinai, they reached for one that fit neatly into the filing cabinet of Greek legal culture. The result? A covenant that sounds suspiciously like a last will and testament. Apparently, Moses needed a notary.

And it doesn't stop there. Their choice of a qualifier διαθησομαι was equally telling. Out of five verbal options, they picked the one that reinforced their noun selection. Coincidence? Hardly. This wasn't just translation, it was theological landscaping. They weren't just planting words, they were reshaping the terrain.

What becomes painfully obvious is the disconnect between the LXX and the Masoretic Text. We need to stop here. Take a breath. Because what the LXX scholars did in Alexandria—for whatever reason—was render Jeremiah in a way that would make a Hebrew prophet blink twice. It's not consistent with its Hebraic context. Nor does it resemble anything from Mesopotamian covenantal norms, which, last I checked, didn't involve probate court.

Instead, the word choices in the LXX follow Greek social and judicial conventions, the kind you'd find in the writings of Solon of Athens, not the thunder of Mount Sinai. The covenant becomes a contract. The divine promise becomes a legal clause. The sacred is filtered through the civic. One might ask: did the translators think Yahweh was running a city-state?

And now, centuries later, we're still living in the shadow of that shift. The theological furniture has been rearranged, and we're sitting in chairs that were never meant to be in the sanctuary. If we're serious about restoring sacred meaning, we must go back, not to the translation, but to the source. Because sometimes, the biggest theological detours begin with a well-intentioned footnote in Greek.

Solon of Athens

According to Solon of Athens (638–558 BCE), the man who gave Athens its legal backbone and apparently moonlighted as Yahweh's estate planner, a διαθήκη (Greek will) came with all the trappings of civic formality. Let's break it down, because the implications are both tragic and unintentionally hilarious.

First, the διαθήκη had to be written. Not thundered from a mountain. Not etched in stone by divine fire. No, it had to be penned, sealed with a signet ring or a signature, and witnessed, presumably by a few bored neighbors who'd rather be at the agora. Sinai, meet bureaucracy.

Second, if there were any issues with the will, say, someone felt they didn't get enough amphorae or goats, they'd take it up with an Archon, a magistrate. Not a prophet. Not a priest. Just your local civic official, probably juggling three inheritance disputes and a zoning complaint. Divine covenant, now available in triplicate.

Third and this is where the comedy writes itself, the recipients of the will could challenge its provisions. That's right. The heirs could march into court and say, "Actually, I think the deity was unclear on clause 4b." Because nothing says sacred promise like litigation.

So when the Septuagint translators chose διαθήκη to render בְּרִית, they weren't just translating, they were rebranding. The covenant became a contested will. YHVH, apparently, needed a legal team and a good pen.

One wonders: did the translators imagine Moses descending Sinai with tablets and a notarized affidavit? Did they picture Jeremiah drafting his prophecies with a legal disclaimer at the bottom? "Terms and conditions apply. Void where prohibited."

This is the theological sleight of hand we're still unpacking. And while the implications are serious, the imagery is almost too rich to ignore. The sacred was put on trial. The covenant was cross-examined. And somewhere in the heavens, a prophet is facepalming.

Upon the Αρειος Παγος, that storied outcrop where Solon, architect of Athenian jurisprudence, once codified the social order, stood Shaul of Tarsus, proclaiming a message that did not pass through the usual channels. No civic preamble. No legal precedent. Just a covenantal summons, thundered into a polis trained to hear only contracts. Really since the time on Mount Tzion maybe God took up a summer home on Mount Olympus.

Was it heard? Truly heard, in the normative lexica of the day? Or did the ears of Athens, dulled by centuries of civic filtration, miss the Hebraic resonance entirely? Was Paul's proclamation received as sacred continuity, or dismissed as philosophical novelty?

And deeper still: was Athens so lexically isolated from the Biblical motifs, from *berit*, from prophetic cadence, from covenantal gravity, that the contextual import of his words failed to register? Did the Areopagites possess the semantic scaffolding to even process what was being offered?

The Perseus Digital Library does supply us with what happened.

Not speculation. Not theological embroidery. Just the raw lexicon, uncurated, unfiltered, and unflinching. It lays bare the semantic terrain of the Greek world, exposing how διαθήκη was used, understood, and, most tellingly, misunderstood.

Category	Details
Greek Word	διαθήκη
Transliteration	*diathēkē*
Meaning (LSJ)	Disposition, arrangement; especially a will or testament. In biblical usage: covenant.
Part of Speech	Noun, singular, feminine
Case & Dialect	Nominative / Vocative; Attic, Epic, Ionic
Lexical Source	LSJ Middle Liddell
Classical Usage	Testamentary will or legal disposition
Biblical Usage	Covenant (translating Hebrew בְּרִית)
Word Frequency (NT)	Appears 33 times
Common Forms	διαθήκη (nom. sg), διαθήκης (gen. sg), διαθήκην (acc. sg), διαθ◇και (nom. pl)
Key NT Verses	Matt 26:28, Heb 9:16–17, Gal 3:15–17

Did the Seventy scholars know that semantics were critical? One would hope so. After all, they weren't scribbling grocery lists, they were commissioned to translate the sacred texts of Israel. Words weren't just tools, they were vessels of covenant, prophecy, and divine fire. So yes, they should have known how a word is used. Especially when the stakes were eternal.

But context matters. And the Jewish community in Alexandria, educated, Hellenized, and perhaps a touch insular, offers a possible explanation. They didn't see their relationship with the God of Avraham as a universal invitation. They saw it as a private club. Membership required lineage, not linguistic clarity.

So when they translated the Hebrew Scriptures into Greek, they weren't building bridges, they were erecting fences. The translation reflects this. It's precise enough to preserve the ritual, but opaque enough to keep outsiders guessing. There was no theological outreach program. No evangelistic footnotes. Just a quiet resolve: *This is ours. You wouldn't understand.*

And the irony? They had returned to Egypt, the land of bondage, voluntarily. Not as slaves, but as scholars. And in their desire to be left alone, they ensured that the Greek-speaking world would be left in the dark. The covenant was rendered in a dialect that preserved mystery, not clarity.

Whatever their reasons, be it cultural pride, theological caution, or linguistic fatigue, we are left with the Septuagint (LXX). A document of profound importance. It shaped the vocabulary of the New Testament, influenced early Church theology, and became the lens through which Gentiles first glimpsed the God of Israel.

But let's not pretend it was neutral. The LXX is not just a translation, it's a theological artifact, forged in the tension between revelation and reservation.

Continuing on with the chronology of translations, we now arrive at a critical juncture, one that demands theological sobriety before we tumble headlong into the proverbial rabbit hole. Two issues must be introduced, and not lightly:

1. **Covenantal** understanding, and
2. **Covenantal** expression, as employed by the authors of subsequent biblical texts.

These are not academic footnotes. They are the hinges upon which the entire theological door swings.

As we've already seen with the advent of the Septuagint, the translation itself introduced a semantic shift, a lexical recalibration that shaped how covenant was perceived, taught, and eventually codified. So before we proceed, these two issues must be addressed with precision. Because where we're headed is not just a discussion of covenant, it's a confrontation with the New **Covenant**.

And the question will not be: *Is there a New Covenant?* That's already assumed. The real question is: Is it consistent with the intent of the prophesied covenant? Does it echo the promises of Jeremiah, the structure of Sinai, the continuity of Avraham? Or does it drift, lexically, theologically, and communally, into something else?

And more pointedly: Does it create a membership status that aligns with the parameters of the covenant in question? Is it grafting or replacing? Is it fulfillment or redefinition? Is it covenantal fidelity or theological innovation?

Because if the New Covenant is built on a mistranslation, the New Testament, a semantic sleight of hand, or a cultural misreading of *berit* as *diathēkē*, then we're not just dealing with doctrinal confusion, we're dealing with a misaligned inheritance.

So before we descend further, let's name the tension. Let's trace the fault lines. And let's ask the question that few dare to ask: Is the New Covenant what the prophets actually saw, or what the translators allowed us to see?

It is precisely here, at the intersection of translation, covenantal intent, and theological drift, that Ephesians 2:11–13 becomes not just relevant, but decisively urgent. This passage is no mere Pauline footnote. It is a covenantal checkpoint, a moment where the eschatological telos the goal, the consummation, the divine trajectory, of membership status is laid bare.

Let's be clear: Paul is not waxing poetic about spiritual proximity. He is declaring a reversal of exclusion, a grafting into the commonwealth of Israel, not a bypass around it.

"You who were once far off..." Not far off from generic spirituality. Far off from covenantal citizenship.

This is not a metaphor. It's a membership transfer, a status realignment, and it hinges on the integrity of the covenantal framework. If the telos of the New Covenant is to bring the nations into Israel's promises, not to overwrite them, then Ephesians 2 is the theological Rosetta Stone. It decodes the eschatological intent. It exposes the ecclesiological sleight of hand. And it demands we ask:

Are we witnessing fulfillment, or theological forgery?

Because if the Gentiles are brought near *to the covenants of promise,* then the covenants themselves must remain intact. No erasure. No replacement. Just proximity through Messiah, not distance through doctrine.

James Barr, no stranger to lexical precision and theological provocation, James Barr was a seminal biblical scholar at Oxford, whose critique of linguistic and theological method reshaped modern exegesis. He is essential to this treatise because he exposed how semantic drift and etymological fallacies distort covenantal meaning—precisely the fractures this work seeks to restore. brought this point to the surface when he wrote:

"Our understanding of how the old and new covenants relate largely determines our understanding of how the Old and New Testaments relate. I "Our understanding of how the old and new covenants relate largely determines our understanding of how the Old and New Testaments relate. I frame the issue this way to highlight the importance of the covenants. Our grasp of the character of the two covenants will have a wide-ranging impact on our grasp of the content of revelation given under those covenants" [21]

Dr. Barr's focus on Paul, particularly his relationship with Moshe and the nature of covenant itself, echoes a question recently posed by Tim Hegg: *"What is 'new' about the New Covenant?"* That question, deceptively simple, is a theological scalpel. Because how one frames the issue at the outset determines not just the trajectory of interpretation, but the integrity of the conclusion. And in this case, the source is no mere human construct, it is a Divine institution, reflecting the character and intent of its Author.

The framing matters. If we begin with a model that assumes rupture, we will end with a theology that celebrates replacement. If we begin with continuity, we will end with fulfillment that honors its foundation. The stakes are not academic, they are covenantal.

Enter E. P. Sanders. His dominance in Pauline studies of late is not just notable, it's definitional. His formulation of *covenantal nomism* has become a crossroads in covenantal understanding, a kind of theological Rosetta Stone that attempts to decode the relationship between Mosaic covenant and New Covenant through the lens of Second Temple Judaism.

Sanders has done more than reframe Paul, he has forced the conversation to confront the nature of grace itself. Not grace as a post-Reformation abstraction, but grace as it functioned within the lived theology of Israel. [22] His challenge is clear: if grace was operative under Moshe, then the New Covenant cannot be defined merely by the arrival of grace, but by its eschatological expansion and internalization.

Because of the current theological climate, or perhaps because this has always been the climate, the most relevant question is not whether God instituted legalism, but whether He ever intended it as the soteriological foundation of the Second Temple period.

Because if He did, then we're not talking about covenantal continuity, we're talking about divine bait-and-switch. And that's precisely how many doctrinal statements frame it: Judaism is law, Christianity is grace. Two religions. Two gods. Two stories. But if that's true, then

Paul's gospel becomes a liberation from the Word of the LORD, a theological jailbreak from the "Old Testament." And Yeshua's identity as Messiah and King of the Jews becomes not just critical, but inconvenient.

So the question remains: What are the actual distinctions between the "old" and "new" covenants?

You often hear statements like "the Old Testament was nailed to the cross." Let's pause. That's not just a misunderstanding of covenant, it's a misunderstanding of God. It implies that older revelation was sinful. That the Torah was a mistake. That Sinai was a setup. Islam takes this notion to its logical extreme: the Torah was corrupted, replaced, discarded. But Paul says otherwise.

Romans 3:31: "Do we then nullify the law through faith? May it never be! On the contrary, we uphold the law." Romans 7:12: "So then, the law is holy, and the commandment is holy and righteous and good."

The problem is not the law. The problem is the lack of context. How many or us are currently part of the 'WE' that uphold the law?, as we just read in Romans 7:12. And that lack has produced the current situation:

- A theological landscape where the Old Testament is treated like a divine misstep,
- Where Marcionite impulses still echo, some groups even denouncing all Scripture except Paul,
- And where the New Covenant is misunderstood as a cosmic reboot rather than a prophetic fulfillment.

How many are part of the 'we So let's ask the obvious: Why would God "make" a covenant to produce a group that already existed? Jews and Gentiles were already on the scene. He's not ratifying their existence. He's certainly not forming a spiritual or physical entity called "the Gentiles." And He's not ending Israel as a covenantal people.

The letter to the Hebrews makes this clear, especially chapters 8 and 10. God is doing something **with** them, not **to** them.

Hebrews 8:10 reads:

"For this is the covenant that I will make *with* the house of Israel after those days, says the Lord: I will put My laws into their minds, and write them on their hearts. And I will be their God, and they shall be My people."

This is not erasure. This is engraving. Not replacement. Renewal. Not contradiction. Fulfillment.

So yes, the writings of the disciples of the Lord Yeshua are relevant, not as a break from the past, but as a bridge. And the question of what is "new" in the New Covenant must be framed not by theological amnesia, but by prophetic continuity.

The next issue, therefore, is the text of the letter to the Hebrews. Written in Koine Greek, yes, but more importantly, it bears the unmistakable imprint of the Septuagint's dominance within the Jewish community of the day. It is certain that Paul, the other disciples, and whoever authored Hebrews were influenced by the LXX. And that influence becomes all the more problematic when we examine Hebrews 8:10 and 10:16.

Why? Because the words διαθήκη (*diathēkē*) and διαθήσομαι (*diathēsomai*) are employed, terms that, in the Greek lexicon, often carry testamentary overtones. Yet the author is clearly presenting a covenantal position, not a last-will-and-testament framework. So what's the issue here?

Are these two verses true? Yes. Are they about a covenant? Linguistically, no. And let me be clear: this is not an attack on the inerrancy of Scripture. It's a recognition of the lexical scaffolding upon which the text was built.

The extant manuscripts of Hebrews, like all translated materials of the time, follow the orthographic and lexicographic patterns of the LXX. That is, they inherit the semantic drift. The covenantal language of בְּרִית (berit) is rendered through the lens of διαθήκη, which in classical Greek often meant a will, not a relational bond.

And this is why I say no, not theologically, but linguistically. To understand these pericopes, you must include Hebrews 9:15–18.

Here, the tension becomes explicit. The author uses testamentary language, death of the one who disposes, validity after death, to illustrate the necessity of Messiah's death. But this does not negate the covenantal thrust of the passage. It's a rhetorical strategy, not a theological redefinition.

As Daniel Gruber writes, the use of διαθήκη in Hebrews 9:15–18 should be understood primarily as "covenant", despite the legal overtones. The author is emphasizing covenantal mediation, not probate court. The inheritance is eternal, not material. The mediator is divine, not civic. He writes:

> "There are several problems with this translation. The first concerns the phrase "the mediator of a new testament" No such thing exists. A mediator is the one who serves to bring agreement or reconciliation between different parties. A testament on the other hand is the declaration of one individual. There is no mediator involved in the solitary issuance of a testament. There can only be a mediator involved when there are two or more parties involved" [23]

I would qualify this statement by noting that in a διαθήκη, or *testamentum*, an Archōn, not a mediator, is only summoned if the validity of the will is challenged in court. And here, two points are painfully obvious, so obvious, in fact, that one wonders how they keep slipping past the theological gatekeepers.

First, we do not see the children of Israel ever challenging the validity of the Covenant. They may have violated it, grieved it, even danced around golden calves in defiance of it, but they never filed a formal objection to its legitimacy. The covenant was never litigated. It was lived, broken, restored, and reaffirmed. And while both Roman and Greek law permitted such a challenge, heirs disputing the terms of a διαθήκη Israel never played that game. Their failure was moral, not procedural.

Second, and more to the point: To challenge the validity of the New Covenant is not merely to contest a clause, it is to abrogate the διαθησομαι itself. And here's the theological earthquake: the διαθησομαι is not a concept. It is a person. It is Messiah Yeshua, in His person and work, who embodies the covenant. The grammar doesn't lie. Both the noun and the verb—*mediation* and *mediator,* are identified with Him. He is not merely the facilitator of divine terms. He is the terms incarnate.

So to challenge the New Covenant is to challenge the Messiah Himself. Not His teachings. Not His followers. Him.

And that, my friend, is not a courtroom dispute. It is a cosmic rebellion. Also, regarding this second issue, the challenge to the validity of the New Covenant, the importance of understanding the covenantal meal must be invoked. Not as a quaint ritual or liturgical footnote, but as a theological linchpin. This is not bread and wine for sentiment's sake. This is blood and body in covenantal function. When we examine the Hebrew text of Exodus, alongside the LXX, the Vulgate, and yes, even the KJV, we find a foundation that is anything but incidental. The textual witnesses converge, sometimes reluctantly, sometimes gloriously, on a pattern that Hebrews 9:12 and Exodus 24:5–6 crystallize.

In Exodus 24, we see sacrificial blood applied to both the altar and the people, a bilateral sealing. And then, what follows? A meal. Not a snack. Not a symbolic gesture. A shared table in the presence of God. The seventy elders beheld Elohim and ate and drank. This is not metaphor. This is covenantal ratification.

Hebrews 9:12 then picks up the thread, not with nostalgic longing, but with eschatological fulfillment. The Messiah enters not by the blood of goats and calves, but by His own blood, securing eternal redemption. The covenantal meal is not abolished, it is elevated. The function remains: blood, presence, communion. But the mediator is now the meal. The priest is now the offering. The covenant is now embodied.

It is here we take a close look at Sh'mot (Exodus) 24:8, the blood-verse par excellence, and its renderings across the linguistic triad: Hebrew, Greek (LXX), Latin (Vulgate), and the 1611 King James Version. Not merely for philological sport, but to trace the covenantal thread that bleeds through translation, tradition, and theological imagination.

Hebrew

ויקח משה את הדם ויזרק על העם ויאמר הנה דם הברית אשר כרת
יהוה עמכם על כל הדברים האלה

Moshe took the blood, and sprinkled it on the people, and said, "Look, this is the blood of the covenant, which the LORD has cut with you concerning all these words."

LXX -- λαβων δε Μωυσης το αιμα κατεσκεδασεν του λαου και ειπεν ιδου το αιμα της διαθηκης ης διεθετο κυριος προς υμας περι παντων των λογων τουτων

Vulgate -- Ille vero sumptum sanguinem respersit in populum, et ait: Hic est sanguis [fœderis] quod [pepigit] Dominus vobiscum super cunctis sermonibus his.

1611 --And Moses tooke the blood and sprinkled it on the people, and said, Behold the blood of the **Couenant** which the Lord hath [**made**] with you, concerning all these words.

Reading the English of Exodus 24:8—especially in its 1611 KJV form, and comparing it to the Greek (LXX), Latin (Vulgate), and the Hebrew original is not a mere exercise in translation trivia. It is the foundation. The contextual scaffolding. The theological soil from which Hebrews 9:12 must be analyzed.

Because once you lay these texts side by side, the comparisons are not just linguistic, they're covenantal motifs. And they demand attention.

- In Hebrew, we have כרת a covenant cut, not signed. Blood thrown, not sprinkled. Sinai was not a ceremony. It was a rupture.
- In the Greek, we get *διεθετο* a covenant arranged, structured, administered. Less visceral, more judicial.
- In the Latin, *pepigit* a covenant ratified, sealed. The language of legal finality.
- And in the KJV, we find "sprinkled" and "made" terms that soften the scene, domesticating the drama for ecclesial digestion.

Then comes Hebrews 9:12, and the author dares to say that Messiah entered not by the blood of goats and calves, but by His own blood, securing eternal redemption.

This is not a new motif. It's a refracted one. The covenantal blood of Exodus is now the foundation, or the umbra of His shadow that are connected with the blood of Messiah. The sprinkled blood becomes the poured-out life. The mediator becomes the offering that which produced the penumbra on display in Exodus.

So yes, the comparisons must be made. And yes, the motifs must be addressed. Because if we fail to trace the covenantal thread from Sinai to גֻּלְגֹּלֶת that is Gulgolet, we risk turning the New Covenant into a theological abstraction—when it was always meant to be a bloody fulfillment.

Regarding the Juxtaposition of Exodus 24 and Hebrews 9: The Intertextual Matrix

The intertextual matrix does not merely suggest itself, it demands recognition. When Exodus 24 and Hebrews 9 are placed in juxtaposition, the echoes are not incidental. They are architectural. Both covenants produce blood that is poured out, sacrifices that are made, and Torah that is imparted. Both require representatives to ascend, to "go up" and receive the covenantal terms. Both culminate in a covenant meal.

This is not contrast. This is pattern. This is template theology.

We are compelled to compare, not to divide. The pericopes do not compete, they converge. The offerings in both are kafar atoning, covering, sealing. And in both, the blood of the covenant is not the covenant itself. It is the ratification. The qualifier. The visible seal of an invisible bond. The words of Yeshua at the so called 'last supper' and the words of Moshe in Exodus 24 are so similiar that they do mirror the other. This is most certainly do to their source being of the LORD himself and therefore of the same religion.

To mistake the blood for the covenant is to confuse means with essence. The covenant is the word, the promise, the relational architecture. The blood is the qualifier, the activator, the ratifying agent.

In Exodus, the blood is thrown *zaraq*, not gently placed. In Hebrews, the blood is entered *dia tou idiou haimatos*, through His own blood. But the function remains: ratification, not replacement. He as High Priest is entering His own house, one made without hands, the same one Moshe saw.

So the matrix becomes evident. Not as a theological upgrade, but as a covenantal continuity. Not as a supersession, but as a sacred echo.

The admonition of 1 Corinthians 11:26 "for as often," **οσακις γαρ αν** , has long sat unbothered, like a clause no one dared cross-examine.

Christendom, in its liturgical fervor, has canonized this into sacrament, embalming it with sacerdotal gravity. But Paul's phrasing is not a liturgical prescription, it's a caveat. A conditional clause. A theological if. Its function is not to sanctify bread into ritual, but to *show the Lord's death*. Not reenact it. Not mystify it. Show it. Display it. Proclaim it. The church, however, has narrowed this to Eucharistic application alone, as though the only valid demonstration of Messiah's death must be choreographed in chalice and wafer. And in every iteration, the emphasis is not on the death itself, but on the eligibility of the participant. The rite has become a gatekeeper, not a witness.

The Exodus 24 Covenant Account at Mt. Sinai

Often called a ceremony, but let us be clear: the word *ceremony* is a theological insertion, not a textual reality. The text itself never uses such language. What we find in Exodus 24:3–11 is not liturgy, it is covenantal enactment, raw and unfiltered.

Let us read it as it stands:

> 3 And Moses came and told the people all the words of the Lord, and all the judgments: and all the people answered with one voice, and said, *All the words which the Lord hath said will we do.* 4 And Moses wrote all the words of the Lord, and rose up early in the morning, and built an altar under the hill, and twelve pillars, according to the twelve tribes of Israel. 5 And he sent young men of the children of Israel, which offered burnt offerings, and sacrificed peace offerings of oxen unto the Lord. 6 And Moses took half of the blood, and put it in basins; and half of the blood he sprinkled on the altar. 7 And he took the book of the covenant, and read in the audience of the people: and they said, *All that the Lord hath said will we do, and be obedient.* 8 And Moses took the blood, and sprinkled it on the people, and said, *Behold the blood of the covenant, which the Lord hath made with you concerning all these words.* 9 Then went up Moses, and Aaron, Nadab, and Abihu, and seventy of the elders of Israel: 10 And they

saw the God of Israel: and there was under his feet as it were a paved work of a sapphire stone, and as it were the body of heaven in his clearness. 11 And upon the nobles of the children of Israel he laid not his hand: also they saw God, and did eat and drink.

Exodus 24:11

Let's be clear: *"They tried to kill us, we survived, let's eat"* may be the unofficial motto of Jewish holidays, but Exodus 24:11 is not its origin story. No one's pulling out brisket and kugel under Sinai's sapphire pavement.

The verse says, *"Yet He did not stretch out His hand against the nobles of the sons of Israel; and they beheld God, and ate and drank."* Sounds peaceful, almost Edenic. But this wasn't a post-trauma nosh, it was a covenantal meal, not a survival buffet. No Amalekites lurking, no Pharaoh in hot pursuit, no Red Sea drama. Just divine presence, sacred ratification, and apparently... table service.

Covenant, Cut and Bound: Not Your Average Testamentum

It might also be noted, though rarely is that as Exodus 24:4 highlights the establishment of God's covenant with the twelve tribes, so too are there twelve apostles prominently seated at that Last Supper in all three synoptics. Coincidence? Only if you think Leonardo da Vinci was painting from a menu instead of a motif.

This is not just a poetic parallel. It's a covenant בְּרִית in both instances. And yes, that's a theological application, but not the kind you'll find in a seminary brochure. Because what Yeshua said at that table wasn't a theological musing. It was legal language. Positional. Binding. You'd be more likely to find it in a law library than a theology department, if they had such a thing. (They don't. They have coffee machines and opinions.)

The timing matters. Yeshua's words were given *before* the Passover, during the preparation for Pesach. Just like Moshe, He was saying the same thing: the blood, the result of a כָּרַת, a cutting was to be in, *with*, *amid* you. Applied. Not theorized. Not spiritualized. Applied.

This blood binds the people with God. It's not a metaphor. It's not a devotional. It's not a footnote in a systematic theology textbook. It's Torah. Instruction. Action. Moshe didn't say, "I have a thought experiment." He took the blood and applied it. That's Exodus 24:8. That's covenantal ratification. That's doing, not debating.

And Yeshua? Same table, same principle. He wasn't hosting a symposium. He was proclaiming a covenant. Hebrews 9:19–20 paraphrases it for clarity: *"He took the blood... and sprinkled both the book itself and all the people."* That's right. Two parties. The Book and the People. Because a covenant is not a solo act. There is no such thing as a one-party covenant. That's called a monologue. Or worse, a theology department.

Now, if בְּרִית were just διαθήκη or Testamenti, we'd have a problem. Because a testament doesn't require two parties. It's a declaration. A publication. It's notarized, not sacrificed. And let's be honest—parchment doesn't bleed. Cut a scroll and you've got a publishing error, not a covenant. (Though yes, publishing companies do set the bleed in the editing process, but that's a bit off topic, unless your covenant is printed in CMYK.)

So let's sum it up:

- **Covenants** require a mediator. testamenta do not.
- **Covenants** are cut. testamenta are published.

And if you remove one party from either scene, Sinai or the Upper Room, you don't just lose the covenant. You lose the people. And that would be a problem for da Vinci. The Convent of Santa Maria delle Grazie just wouldn't be the same. Twelve empty chairs and a loaf of bread. Not exactly sacred drama.

This covenant is both simple and complex. It's blood and binding. It's not a theological issue. It's a legal one. And it's not optional.

Dead Men Don't Mediate: A Diatheke Dilemma

Let's not miss the obvious: both διαθήκη and Testamenti begin with the death of the *testator*, not the *mediator*. That's not just a semantic distinction, it's a theological landmine. Because if the covenant is framed as a testament, then the one who mediates it must first die to activate it. Which is fine, until someone tries to dispute it. Then what?

In the case of a διαθήκη, if the terms are contested, the proper recourse would be to call in an ◇ρχων a magistrate, a legal authority. Not a priest. Not a prophet. A bureaucrat. Which is already a downgrade.

And as for a Testamenti, well, a mediator can only be summoned if the provisions are challenged in court. Which makes for an interesting turn of events, considering the mediator has already died. Good luck cross-examining a corpse. The judge might ask, "Is the testator present?" and the bailiff would reply, "Not unless you count the empty tomb."

This is the theological equivalent of trying to renegotiate a contract with someone who's no longer on payroll. You can't call the mediator back into the room, He's ascended. And if you do, you're not mediating. You're resurrecting. Which, to be fair, Yeshua did. But that's not how Roman law works.

So let's be clear: if your covenantal framework depends on the death of the testator to activate the terms, you've already lost the relational thread. Because a בְּרִית doesn't wait for death, it's ratified in blood, yes, but it's enacted in life. It binds *living* parties. It demands presence, not probate.

And if you're still trying to fit that into a theology department, you might want to check the syllabus. Or better yet, the obituary section.

One Message, One Mediator, One Time

Let's dispense with the fragmentation. The Sinai covenant and the New Covenant are not rival pamphlets stapled together by divine indecision. They are linked, structurally, theologically, and narratively. And more to the point: they are one-time events.

At Sinai, Moshe *sprinkled blood on the people*. Not once before. Not once after. That moment was singular, unrepeatable, covenantal. It wasn't a ritual—it was a ratification.

Likewise, the Mediator of the New Covenant does not die repeatedly like some liturgical groundhog day. He dies **once**. *Hebrews 9:28* is not vague: "Christ was offered once to bear the sins of many." *I Peter 3:18* doubles down: "Christ also suffered once for sins, the righteous for the unrighteous." The Greek doesn't stutter. The grammar doesn't allow for sequels.

So let's not pretend we're dealing with two disconnected dramas. There is one senior author behind both events, one divine signature across both covenants. The blood at Sinai and the death at Calvary are not competing symbols. They are echoes. One message, not two.

To suggest otherwise is to turn covenant into collage. But the sacred text resists scissors. It demands continuity. It demands coherence. And it demands that we stop treating the Mediator like a revolving door.

This is all together confirmed by the words of Hebrews 9:14. This verse:

πόσω μαλλον το αιμα του χριστου ος δια πνευματος αιωνιου εαυτον προσηνεγκεν αμωμον τω θεω καθαριει την συνειδησιν υμων απο νεκρων εργων εις το λατρευειν θεω ζωντι

The use of πόσω μαλλον is to declare a difference in degree, not of kind. For there are two ways in which a difference can be made, one of degree and one of kind. To imply they are different in kind would disparage God's commands to Israel as either pointless or wrong. On the contrary it would be demanding that the greater sacrifice be made, the Sacrifice that was the source of the revelation in Exodus and Levitius. To imply that the sacrifices in the Tenach were at best ineffectual is to say that:

a. all of Israel was unatoned for

b. God was misleading them.

To the extent to which the sacrifices were atoning is not the point. Their purpose was no more invalid than they will be in the Millenium, in the Temple described by Ezekiel. The Priesthood is at issue in Hebrews, not the covenant. This is where the translators deliberately are misleading. When they insert the word 'covenant' into Hebrews 8:7,13; 9:1. His Priesthood is different in 'manor', namely that of Melchi Tzedek. Which is not to say that its demands were not the same. The Blood and the Word are the same. The Torah, the Prophets and the Ketuvim Hadereck, the writings of the way, all agree - Leviticus 17:11; Ezekiel 43:18 and Hebrews 9:22

Through a Glass Dimly—Or Just Through a Fog of Our Own Making?

The notion that we're peering "through a glass dimly" is not entirely Paul's fault. Some of the haze is of our own making—smudged by centuries of ecclesial fingerprints and theological grease. Take Romans 15:16, for example. The phrase was popularized by John Wesley and George Whitefield, who used it to instantiate the now-ubiquitous title: *"ministers of the gospel."* A phrase which, let's be honest, sounds official, sounds reverent, and sounds... completely unscriptural.

Yes, you read that right. The phrase *"minister(s) of the gospel"* does not appear anywhere in Scripture. Not once. There are only three instances where the word *minister* appears in the singular, and none in the plural. Which makes you wonder how we ended up with entire denominations built on a title that never made it past the editorial board of the Holy Spirit.

Now, this isn't to preclude its prior use by Catholic and Orthodox traditions to bolster their own sacramental authority. They've been playing ecclesiastical chess for centuries. But let's not pretend the Protestants didn't bring their own fog machine to the party.

And what of the gospel itself? It means *"good news."* But surely we're not relegated to humming Bobby McFerrin's *Don't Worry, Be Happy* as our liturgical anthem. The gospel is not a mood, it's a message. And if we don't know who we are and what we're a part of, we might want to hold off on speaking altogether. Otherwise, we risk becoming part of the problem.

This includes the Messianic movement, by the way. As a sincere attempt to return to the contextual message of the first *people of the way*, they are not exempt from delivering that message with clarity. Restoration is not a hall pass for ambiguity.

Because if we all keep fumbling the transmission, we'll end up crying:

"What we have here is a failure to communicate." -- *Cool Hand Luke*, 1967

And that's not just cinematic. That's prophetic.

It would be not only appropriate but theologically responsible to include the Targumim and the Peshitta in this chapter, perhaps as an addendum, perhaps as a quiet footnote that refuses to stay quiet. These are not distant echoes; they are contemporaneous witnesses, breathing the same historical air as the early rabbinic and apostolic communities. Their proximity is not incidental, it is providential. To have two other traditions forming so close in time is not a complication; it is a gift. A triangulation. A challenge to monoculture.

More than a century ago, Milton S. Terry, that rare Protestant who dared to read eastward, argued for the inclusion of the Targums in Christian theological reflection. Not as exotic artifacts, but as living connections to Jewish theological thought. Yes, they are geographically and communally bounded. Yes, they speak with accents shaped by Babylon and Galilee. But they illustrate, they illuminate, and they interrupt, which is precisely what good theology should do.

As Terry wrote, with the kind of clarity that makes modern footnotes blush:

"The best ancient Jewish exegesis is represented in the Targums of Onkelos and Ben Uzziel. These are the Chaldee paraphrases of the Pentateuch and the Prophets. The Targum of Onkelos on the Pentateuch is of great value as a translation. It is in the main a tolerably faithful rendering of the Hebrew, and its occasional explanatory additions are usually worthy of attention and regard."

"Tolerably faithful", a phrase that deserves its own commentary. For in those explanatory additions, we find not just linguistic glosses but theological instincts. Instincts that predate councils and creeds. Instincts that still whisper across the parchment.

To exclude these texts would be to silence voices that were never meant to be silent. Let them speak. Let them color the margins. Let them remind us that sacred meaning was never meant to be monopolized.

In this stream of thought, one of the most compelling efforts currently underway is the work of Duane D. Miller, PhD, a scholar who refuses to let the Aramaic roots of theology remain buried under Greek gloss. His recent study on the Aramaic term מֵימְרִי (*Memri*) is not just linguistic archaeology; it's theological excavation. He proposes, with precision and boldness, that *Memri* is foundational to understanding the Greek Logos and the English Word, not as a philosophical abstraction, but as a Jewish theological reality.

Miller doesn't merely gesture toward Jewish context; he anchors John 1:1 within it. He demonstrates that the prologue of John is not a Hellenistic hymn floating in Platonic ether, but a midrashic echo, firmly situated within the Jewish community, resonating with Parsha Lech Lecha and the calling of Avraham. This is not incidental. It's intentional. It's covenantal.

I highly recommend his work, not just for its scholarship, but for its courage. His commentary, recently published, is a must-read. And his website - https://www.matsati.com/

What is the outcome of all this? We will see its fruit in what occurred, in the following chapters.

Three

The Mystery of Lawlessness

"If this were play'd upon a stage now, I could condemn it as an improbable fiction." [25]

The Apostolic Fathers are identified not by apostolic charisma or prophetic fire, but by the extant texts to which a direct or indirect connection with the Apostles is indicated. That is: we have letters, fragments, and theological echoes, some clear, some distorted, preserved like ancient radio signals bouncing off the canyon walls of early orthodoxy. So the question arises, and not politely:

Did they forward the message of the New Covenant, or did they begin its domestication?

Magnus Zetterholm's identification of the problem is critical, not because he solves it, but because he dares to ask it without genuflecting to consensus. Associate Professor of New Testament Studies at Lund University's Centre for Theology and Religious Studies. His query, stripped of academic varnish, is this:

> "If the Jesus movement started out as a Jewish messianic faction, how can it be explained that a representative of the same movement, about a eighty years later, finds the basic religious outlook of Judaism to be incompatible with the same movement he represents?" [26]

Qualifying the statement with "if," as Zetterholm did, I propose, be viewed not as epistemic caution but as rhetorical accommodation, for the sake of those who are the objects of this outlook: namely, the αιρεσεως of Acts 24:5, the specific sect of the Nazarenes. Not a generic fringe group. Not a theological aberration. A sect within Judaism, as Acts 5:17; 15:5; 24:14; and 26:5 make abundantly clear.

This is not a movement that broke away from Judaism. It is a movement that broke open its prophetic fulfillment. Here the word translated as sect as Acts 28:22 confirms the category: "concerning this sect, we know that it is spoken against everywhere." Sectarian, yes, but not severed. The Nazarenes were not apostates from Torah; they were its eschatological witnesses. So we must ask, without flinching:

At what point was the content of the New Covenant withdrawn? More to the point:

By what legerdemain was the Torah removed from the New Covenant?

Was it sleight of hand? A rhetorical flourish? It is clear that for most of Christendom, the statement:

$$\underline{τελος}\ γαρ\ νομου\ χριστος\ εις\ δικαιοσυνην\ παντι\ τω\ πιστευοντι\ -$$
Romans 10:4

Within this quintessential pericope, the τελος as a morpheme "stood apart" from the Messianic intent—not for linguistic reasons, but theological ones. It was cordoned off, quarantined, lest its natural trajectory disrupt the preferred narrative.

Of all the possible lexical usages, goal, fulfillment, consummation, the one that has been ruled out is the very one its lemma would demand. The one most consistent with Matthew 5:17, where the Messiah explicitly states he did not come to abolish the Law or the Prophets, but to fulfill them.

As Negation of the Torah: A Misuse of Matthew 5:17

The irony is almost liturgical.

The very verse that begins with *Μη νομισητε* "Do not think" has become the cornerstone of precisely that: a theological misthinking. Matthew 5:17, in which Yeshua explicitly denies any intent to *καταλυσαι* (dismantle, abolish, nullify) the Torah or the Prophets, has been wielded—absurdly—as a tool to do just that. The negation of negation has become the affirmation of erasure.

Let's be clear: this is not a semantic slip. It is a paradigmatic inversion.

The phrase *ουκ ηλθον καταλυσαι αλλα πληρωσαι* ("I did not come to abolish but to fulfill") has been contorted into a theological sleight of hand, where "fulfill" is redefined not as *embodying, enacting*, or *bringing to fullness*, but as *rendering obsolete*. In this twisted logic, fulfillment becomes termination, and continuity becomes rupture. It is curious—no, it is astonishing, that in light of Yeshua's own statement, in which He uses the words abolish (*καταλυσαι*) and fulfill (*πληρωσαι*), readers cannot seem to acknowledge that these are polar opposites.

Not adjacent. Not synonymous. Not interchangeable. Opposites.

To abolish is to dismantle. To fulfill is to complete. One tears down; the other builds up. One discards; the other confirms. And yet, in much of Christian theology, these two have been made to shake hands, like fire and water agreeing to coexist.

Thus, the verse meant to safeguard the covenantal provision has been weaponized to object to it. The often denial of this by even Evangelical groups fails to account for why nearly all the English translations of *τελος* is 'the end' in Romans 10:4

This is not exegesis. It is exorcism, of Torah's sacred rhythm, of prophetic continuity. It is the theological equivalent of declaring a marriage fulfilled and therefore annulled.

But Yeshua's words do not permit such gymnastics. He does not whisper ambiguity. He thunders clarity. *Do not think*, because he knew we would.

And we did. I did as well during the time I spent as a dispensationalist.

Covenantal Provisions the Noahide Laws?

The 'Messianic' movement to which I am apart is not immune from this predicament. It has divided the movement.

The *Messianic* movement is not immune from this predicament. Far from it. It has, in fact, been divided by it. The fragmentation is not merely theological, it's existential. The messianic denominations are the result of both an internal identity crisis and an external projection of who they are supposed to be. And mostly, they've failed to do either of the following:

- Acknowledge the New Covenant
- Or agree on its soteriological mechanism

Some dispute its terms. Others dispute its existence. And still others treat it like a theological heirloom, precious, but not particularly useful.

For many, the question of an organic connection between Acts 15 and the later Noahide laws, codified in the Tosefta by rabbinic Judaism, seems relevant, especially in a chapter about lawlessness. Because if Acts 15 is merely proto-Noahide, then Gentile inclusion is not covenantal, it's regulatory. It's not grafting, it's licensing.

Cue the quote:

> "For a Tanna of the School of Manasseh taught: The sons of Noah were given seven precepts, viz., [prohibition of] idolatry, murder, robbery, flesh cut from a living animal, emasculation and forbidden mixtures." —Sanhedrin 56b, Babylonian Talmud

If this were the case, it's no wonder a covenant status is employed. The Noahide covenant has become a theological placeholder, used in Protestantism for the same reason it's used in Judaism: to explain Gentile inclusion without requiring covenantal continuity. But the charge of anachronism looms large.

Let's ask the obvious questions:

1. Where were the Gentiles given these laws? (Spoiler: not in Genesis.)
2. In what languages were these laws given? (Aramaic? Akkadian? Proto-Noahide Esperanto?)
3. Exactly when did the sons of Noah first read Sanhedrin 56b? (Before or after the printing press?)
4. How is it that the eight parties listed in Genesis 9:8–10 were reduced to one? (Did someone misplace the other seven?)

The reduction of covenantal plurality to a single generic category "the sons of Noah" is not just a theological oversimplification. It's a narrative collapse. Genesis 9 lists eight parties. The Noahide framework lists one. That's not continuity. That's editorial compression.

The Rainbow Connection: Not Just for Amphibians

Let's start with the text. Not the tradition. Not the extrapolation. The Torah.

The eight parties to the covenant in Genesis 6 and 9 are not speculative—they are listed:

1. Noach – Genesis 6:18; 9:8
2. His sons – same verses
3. His wife – Genesis 6:18
4. His sons' wives – Genesis 6:18
5. Their descendants – Genesis 9:9, 12
6. Birds – Genesis 6:20; 9:10
7. Cattle – Genesis 9:10
8. Beasts of the earth – Genesis 9:10

This is not metaphor. This is covenantal roll call.

And this covenant is qualified, not by legislation, but by a sign: קַשְׁתִּי *My bow*, the rainbow. A visual token, not a legal code. A promise, not a penal system.

Nowhere in these chapters are laws mentioned. Not one. If there were, then all eight parties would be bound to observe them. Including the birds. Including the beasts. Including the cattle. Unless someone's prepared to install a rabbinic court in the barnyard, we might want to reconsider the premise.

So by what mechanics could this covenant be not applicable to the Jews, who are, by definition, descendants of Noah? Are we to imagine that the Jewish people opted out of the rainbow clause? That they were grandfathered into a different covenantal jurisdiction?

Do we really think the Jewish people would, or could, join Kermit the Frog in singing *The Rainbow Connection*? Especially if the Gentiles violated this covenant and the birds were held accountable?

Let's look at the Noahide laws as listed in the Shulchan Aruch [27]:

1. Prohibition of Idolatry – You shall not have any idols before God.
2. Prohibition of Murder – You shall not murder. (Genesis 10?)
3. Prohibition of Theft – You shall not steal.
4. Prohibition of Sexual Promiscuity – You shall not commit adultery.
5. Prohibition of Blasphemy – You shall not blaspheme God's name.
6. Prohibition of Cruelty to Animals – Do not eat flesh from a living animal.
7. Requirement to Establish Just Laws – You shall set up a judiciary to enforce the above.

Now ask yourself:

- Where are these laws in Genesis 6 or 9?

- In what language were they given?
- When did the sons of Noah first read Sanhedrin 56b?
- And how did the covenantal scope of eight parties shrink to one generic category?

This is not covenantal continuity. It's theological compression. The Noahide covenant, as popularly taught, is not a textual reality, it's a post-biblical construct retrofitted to solve Gentile relation problems without invoking grafting, blood, or covenantal fidelity.

But Genesis doesn't play along. The rainbow is not a law. It's a sign. And the covenant includes birds. Good luck enforcing adultery statutes on the sparrows.

The Noahide Covenant: A Red Herring in Technicolor

This covenant Genesis 9 is between God and whom?

Let's be honest. Can an animal commit idolatry, murder, theft, adultery, blasphemy, or cruelty to other animals? Can it establish just laws?

I mean, apart from a certain scene in *The Lion King*

So we have a problem. Actually, three.

1. There Is But One Law

The Torah is explicit:

- Exodus 12:49 – *"One law shall be for the native and for the stranger."*
- Numbers 15:15–16 – *"One statute... one ordinance... one law."*
- Leviticus 24:22 – *"You shall have the same law for the stranger and for one from your own country."*

This is not a footnote. It's a refrain. And it's recited daily in the Shacharit Service, ninth stanza of the Yigdal.[28]

There is no bifurcation. No Gentile clause. No Noahide appendix.

2. No Provision for Separate Atoning

There is no sacrificial system for Noahides. No priesthood. No altar. No blood. And without blood, there is no atoning. Hebrews 9:22 agrees: *"Without the shedding of blood, there is no forgiveness."*

So if Gentiles are relegated to a separate category, they are also excluded from the mechanism of atoning. That's not inclusion. That's theological exile.

3. The Noahide Covenant Is a Classic Red Herring

It marginalizes the New Covenant at best. But its real intent is to nullify it. To replace grafting with categorization. To substitute covenantal intimacy with regulatory distance.

And this brings us to its obvious conflict in Acts 15.

Because Acts 15 is not a Noahide checklist. It is a covenantal negotiation. The apostles are not codifying rabbinic tradition, they are discerning how Gentiles are to be included, not segregated. The four prohibitions listed are not Noahide laws, they are entry points, not exit strategies.

To invoke the Noahide covenant as a solution to Gentile inclusion is to miss the point entirely. It's not a bridge. It's a bypass.

Jerusalem Council: Narrative, Prophetic, and the Pivot of Acts 15:19
The Council of Jerusalem (Acts 15:6–29) is not a sterile doctrinal decree. It's a narrative negotiation, a theological wrestling match in real time. The apostles are not issuing edicts from ivory towers, they are responding to a seismic shift already underway.

1. Anecdotal Evidence First

Barnabas and Paul speak not as theorists but as eyewitnesses. Acts 15:12–14: They recount signs, wonders, conversions, Gentiles turning not toward a Noahide framework, but toward the God of Israel. Not toward abstraction, but toward covenantal reality.

This is not speculative theology. It's empirical testimony.

2. Then Prophetic Authority

They don't stop at anecdotes. They anchor their case in Scripture:

- Amos 9:11 – *"I will rebuild the fallen tent of David."*
- Psalm 22:27 – *"All the ends of the earth shall remember and turn to the Lord."*
- Zechariah 8:23 – *"Ten men from the nations... will grasp the garment of a Jew."*

These are not peripheral texts. They are covenantal prophecies—not of parallel systems, but of Gentile grafting into Israel's restoration.

3. The Pivot: Acts 15:19

Everything turns on this verse:

"Therefore I judge that we should not trouble those from among the Gentiles who are turning to God."
Greek: εθνων επιστρεφουσιν επι τον θεον

This is not future tense. It's present participle. The Gentiles are already turning, actively, presently, covenantally.

This is not a theoretical allowance. It's a recognition of reality. The turning is not toward a diluted ethic or a seven-point checklist. It is toward the God of Israel, toward His covenant, toward His people.

The Council is not inventing inclusion. It's acknowledging it.

Acts 15: The Turning, the Teaching, and the Trouble with Noahide Theology

For the peoples who are turning επιστρεφουσιν the grammar speaks louder than the commentaries. It is a present tense active participle, not a hypothetical future, not a conditional clause. These Gentiles are already in motion. The turning is underway. The Council is not initiating it—they are responding to it.

And what follows is not ambiguity. It's structure.

- Verse 20 gives content - a distilled message, not a full Torah scroll, but a starting point.
- Verse 21 gives context - the mechanism by which this message is received.

The conjunction γάρ is not filler. It is a particle of affirmation, a theological hinge. It affirms that Moshe is read on the Shabbat, and not in abstract. In synagogues. Among Gentiles. The process is already in motion.

This is where Gary Beresford's observation becomes critical. The word γενεων "of generations" is neuter genitive plural. It is not addressing a specific ethnic group. It is describing a transgenerational reality. The Gentiles in question are not random passersby. They are already present in the synagogue. Already listening. Already turning.

And yet, apparently no one asked why these Gentiles were in the synagogue in the first place. Were they tourists? Curious pagans? Or were they seekers, drawn by the voice of Moshe, echoing through the Shabbat readings?

Before we can move on to the Apostolic and Patristic writings, we must confront the theological detour known as the Noahide laws.

- Was the early Messianic community influenced by halakhah, as Mark Nanos has suggested?
- Was the rabbinical view the deus ex machina that emerged from the Jerusalem Council?
- Were the disciples secretly referencing the Book of Jubilees?
- Or were they shaped by the voice of Jeremiah, who spoke of a New Covenant written on the heart?

The reality is this: Acts 15 did not settle the eschatological status of Gentiles. It acknowledged their turning. It offered a provisional framework. But it did not define their covenantal endpoint. And yet, many modern scholars have inverted the theology. They would make the Jews the problem, as if the covenantal people were the obstacle to Gentile inclusion, rather than the root into which Gentiles are grafted. This is not just bad theology. It's theological revisionism. It turns the olive tree upside down, and calls it progress, though definitely not low hanging fruit.

Apostolic Authors: Naming the Nameless. By the time Ignatius of Antioch, was an early Christian bishop, was penning his epistles, the term Christianity had become so colloquial, so liturgically lacquered, that one might assume it was the dominant refrain of the apostolic canon itself. Listen to any homily today and you'd be forgiven for thinking the word Christian was etched into every scroll and syllable of Scripture. It wasn't.

Not once did a member of the believing community refer to themselves as Christian in the Biblical texts. The term appears, yes, but always from the outside looking in. A label affixed by others. A name given, not claimed. And yet, this lexical orphan has been adopted, baptized, and enthroned as though it were the cornerstone of faith itself.

Some theologians, those brave enough to squint at the text without the fog of tradition, acknowledge this. But acknowledgment without consequence is ecclesial theater. The tragedy is not merely semantic. It is covenantal.

Today, the interaction between Jew and Gentile is staged under the rubric of conversion, a term that should be anathema to anyone who has read the prophets with their eyes open. The fulfillment of prophecy has been severed from the issuance of prophecy, as though the vine could flourish without the root.

Many Gentiles, in their zeal, believe Jews must be converted, as if the prophets of Israel were prophets of the church. They were not. They spoke to, for, and within Israel. Their words were not ecclesial forecasts but covenantal declarations. To suggest otherwise is to rewrite the script mid-performance and call it divine improvisation.

What the children of Israel need is not conversion, but confirmation, that their prophets were right. That the promises spoken in Hebrew were not annulled in Greek. That the grafting in of Gentiles was not a hostile takeover but a horticultural miracle.

God never named the religion. Man did that. And every time we mistake the name for the covenant, we trade sacred continuity for ecclesial branding.

Returning to the Apostolic Fathers they are generally listed by manuscripts not necessarily by names.

These are:

Citations of Pre Nicaean Covenants References
The Apostolic Fathers Greek Texts with English translations of their writings.

You will see below a chart cataloguing the uses of διαθηκης and διαθησομαι, terms not merely lexical, but covenantal arteries pulsing through divine intent. Excepting I Clement and Barnabas, the Will and its Publishing are conspicuously absent. Not misquoted. Not misapplied. Simply not there. Thus, no attempt is made to relay the message, even in its incorrect form. The silence is not distortion; it is omission. And omission, in this case, speaks louder than error. In fact there are no known from Hebrews chapters 8 or 10 in these manuscripts. What is obvious is that, with the exception of I Clement the message of the New Covenant was not transmitted in this period. Even though Clement of Rome, Fourth bishop of Rome, was aware of it. He did write:

'Being adorned with a virtuous and honorable manner of life, you performed all your duties in the fear of him The Commandments and the ordinances of the Lord were "written on the tablets of your hearts' [29]

Work	Date	Genre	διαθηκης	διαθησομαι
1 Clement	ca. 96	Letter	15.4; 34.4	None
Epistle of Barnabas	ca. 130	Letter	4.7; 4.8 (×2); 6.19; 9.6; 9.9; 13.1; 13.6; 14.2; 14.3; 14.5; 14.7	10.2
2 Clement	ca. 150	Sermon	None	None
Didache	ca. 50–70	Manual	None	None
Epistle of Polycarp	ca. 130	Letter	None	None
Shepherd of Hermas	ca. 150	Allegory	None	None
Martyrdom of Polycarp	ca. 69–100	Narrative	None	None

Work	Date	Genre	διαθηκης	διαθησομαι
Ignatius (Letters)	d. 117	Ephesians Magnesians Trallians Philadelphians Smyrnaeans Polycarp	None	None

Several points can be made here, none of them flattering. Both Christendom and Judaism would nod in agreement at the absence of New Covenant instructions in the Apostolic Fathers, not because they understand the omission, but because it conveniently mirrors their current theological positions: namely, that there is no consistency. The silence suits them. It spares them the burden of coherence.

Both camps are complicit in the separation of the communities. Christendom, with its triumphalist supersessionism, and Judaism, with its quiet insistence on Gentile distance, have conspired, perhaps unintentionally, perhaps not, to deny the covenantal status proposed in Romans 11 and Ephesians 1:5; 2:13. The "new man" of Ephesians 2 is not a metaphor for ecclesial diversity. It is a covenantal grafting, a horticultural miracle. It infers terms like εγγυς εγενηθητε (*you were brought near*) in *Ephesians 2:13*, ενεκεντρισθης (*you were grafted in*) in Romans *11:17*, and υιοθεσιαν (*adoption*) in *Ephesians 1:5*, each a theological scalpel cutting through centuries of tribalism.

The Church denies inclusion with Israel. Judaism prefers isolation. One says, "You are not us." The other says, "Please don't be." And yet the Gentiles, those απηλλοτριωμενοι (*alienated ones*) of *Ephesians 2:12*, are described not as invaders, but as scions. Wild olive branches. Not native, but not disposable. The grafting metaphor is not ornamental; it is ontological.

Ironically, the Church views the Jews as the aliens. One wonders what would happen if Israel pulled the ultimate theological troll and landed a UFO in Rome with Hebraic markings ablaze, just to remind the Church who wrote the scrolls. The theological problem of Ephesians 2:11 is embedded in the clause: οτι υμεις ποτε τα εθνη "that you were once Gentiles." If that was then, what are you now? Have the Gentiles joined Israel in covenantal statehood? Have the two become the "one new man"? Or is the phrase just ecclesial wallpaper?

Now I must address an all-too-common theological position. I will present the concise statement, not because it is correct, but because it is popular:

> "Paul explained that Gentiles who were 'aliens... of Israel, and strangers from the covenants of promise' have been 'made nigh (to God) by the blood of Christ.' God has broken down the middle wall of partition (between Jew and Gentile); having abolished in his flesh the (Mosaic) Law of commandments contained in ordinances; for to make himself of twain (Jew and Gentile) one new man." —*Ephesians 2:13–22, name withheld.*

This notion is a tragedy. It omits the enmity την εχθραν as the thing being broken down, not the Law. The enmity is abolished. Not Torah. This is not a semantic quibble; it is a theological pivot. Verse 16 repeats and clarifies: "putting to death the enmity." It does not read "putting to death the Law." The Law is not the villain. The parsing of clauses and phrases in OpenText.org [30] and the work of *Dr. William D. Ramsey* [31] confirm this. The source material is sound. The interpretation, however, has been hijacked.

Technical Alert: The direct object of καταργήσας must land somewhere. It has two possible targets:

1. την εχθραν, with τον νομον in apposition - i.e., "by abolishing in His flesh the enmity," where the Law is the context, not the casualty.

2. τον νομον, taking την εχθραν in apposition

So stop already saying it! Who is your master? Because we know who you're quoting. This was stated directly by Norman L. Geisler:

> "But in Christ the Law is fulfilled (*Romans 8:2*) and done away with." [32]

Done away with? Really? The one law the Church seems willing to accept is the law of unintended consequences. And if you're going to argue that the Apostles endorsed this, I'll need to see the words Ωχ [33] or Αμαν [34] in their writings, because that's the only way this theological facepalm gets canonical approval. The tragedy is not that the Church misunderstood Paul. The tragedy is that it preferred the misunderstanding.

When the Messiah reiterated Moshe's declaration *"Man does not live by bread alone, but by every word that proceeds out of the mouth of God"* He wasn't just quoting Scripture. He was issuing a proclamation. A covenantal ultimatum. And both Christianity and Judaism have politely refused to live by it.

Let's be clear: they were saying the same thing. Moshe and Messiah. Torah and Incarnation. But the response? A theological shrug.

Judaism rejects the writings of the Apostles and Disciples. Christianity refuses to live by the Tenach. So neither accepts **all** of the Word. Each has curated their canon to suit their comfort. Christianity could avoid the tension by simply declaring that the "Old Testament" is not the Word of God. Problem solved. If it's not divine, you don't have to obey it. Convenient.

The irony? Judaism has long accepted the adage: *"When Messiah comes, He will teach us how to live out Torah properly."* This presupposes that Torah is not currently being lived out properly. That Messiah will need to correct Halacha. That the rabbinic scaffolding will need divine renovation.

So let me ask: who is worse off?

Christianity, which denies the foundation? Or Judaism, which admits the foundation is cracked but insists on building anyway?

Either way, the proclamation stands: *"By every word..."* Not some. Not the ones we like. Not the ones that fit our denominational branding. Every word.

On to Apostolic Devices. How the early believers saw themselves, first in the Apostolic period, then through the Ante-Nicene era, formed the backdrop for the Ecumenical Councils and Creeds. Their self-perception wasn't just theological; it was architectural. They were building something. And the blueprint wasn't Scripture, it was structure.

Of the Apostolic Fathers, generally numbered from five to eight, one must ask: *Were they forwarding the message of Yeshua?* Were they united by a common benchmark, one that resembled the Priests and Prophets of Israel?

The answer, if we're honest, is no. Not in voice. Not in posture. Not in covenantal fidelity.

The Priests and Prophets of Israel were not institutional mascots. They were covenantal guardians. They spoke with fire, wept with burden, and stood between the people and their God. Their benchmark was not ecclesial structure, it was divine instruction. Torah was not a footnote; it was the foundation.

The Apostolic Fathers, by contrast, were often more concerned with polity than prophecy. Their unity was not forged in covenantal continuity, but in ecclesial survival. They quoted Yeshua, yes—but did they walk as He walked? Did they echo the prophetic cadence of Amos, Isaiah, Jeremiah? Or did they trade the mantle for a mitre?

The benchmark they shared was not the one handed down at Sinai. It was the one drafted in councils. And while some, like Clement and Barnabas—show flickers of covenantal awareness, the overall trajectory veers toward institutional consolidation, not prophetic restoration.

So were they forwarding the message of Yeshua? Only if that message was reduced to creedal assent and hierarchical allegiance. But if the message was *"Follow Me"* in life, in law, in love, then the benchmark was missed.

Thematic Overlaps and Emphases Among the Eight Apostolic Fathers

Apostolic Fathers	Church Order	Martyrdom	Christology	Ethics	Eschatology	Jewish-Christian Relations	Sacraments	Scripture Interpretation	Unity	Mission
Clement of Rome	0.37	0.95	0.73	0.60	0.16	0.16	0.06	0.87	0.60	0.71
Ignatius of Antioch	0.02	0.97	0.83	0.21	0.18	0.18	0.30	0.52	0.43	0.29
Polycarp of Smyrna	0.61	0.14	0.29	0.37	0.46	0.79	0.20	0.51	0.59	0.05
Papias of Hierapolis	0.61	0.17	0.07	0.95	0.97	0.81	0.30	0.10	0.68	0.44
Barnabas	0.12	0.50	0.03	0.91	0.26	0.66	0.31	0.52	0.55	0.18
Hermas	0.97	0.78	0.94	0.89	0.60	0.92	0.09	0.20	0.05	0.33
Didache	0.39	0.27	0.83	0.36	0.28	0.54	0.14	0.80	0.07	0.99
Epistle to Diognetus	0.77	0.20	0.01	0.82	0.71	0.73	0.77	0.07	0.36	0.12

Themes

What the Map Reveals
- Shared Themes:

  - Christology, Ethics, and Unity are widely emphasized, suggesting a common concern for moral formation and doctrinal coherence.
  - Church Order and Scriptural Interpretation also show strong overlap, especially among Clement, Ignatius, and the Didache.
- Distinctive Voices:

- ○ Hermas leans heavily into Eschatology and Sacraments, with visionary and allegorical content.
- ○ Barnabas and the Epistle to Diognetus emphasize Jewish-Christian Relations, often polemically.
- ○ Papias remains unique in his oral tradition-based Scripture Interpretation and millennial Eschatology.
- ○ The Didache stands out for its practical focus on Ethics, Mission, and Sacraments.

It should be noted *with no small measure of astonishment* that among the themes preserved by the so-called Apostolic Fathers, the Covenant that was "cut" by Yeshua is conspicuously absent. Not misinterpreted. Not diluted. Simply not included.

This is no minor omission. This is the theological equivalent of forgetting the wedding while cataloging the reception. The Brit Hadashah, the New Covenant in His blood, was not a metaphor. It was a fulfillment, a grafting, a sealing, a restoration. And yet, in the writings of these early ecclesial voices, it is treated as if it were either too Jewish to mention or too inconvenient to preserve. In addition it should also be noted that regarding the issue of Yeshua's atoning on our behalf, this is supplanted by the implementing of the sacraments.

It should also be noted *with equal gravity* that none of them ever used the actual name given to the Messiah by Miryam and Yosef at birth. Not once. Not in passing. Not in reverence. Not even when engaging Jewish interlocutors. The name Yeshua, rich with meaning, rooted in Hebrew promise *"salvation"* is replaced by transliterations and titles that, while later canonized, sever the linguistic thread that ties Him to Israel's hope.

This is not mere semantics. This is identity erasure. The name Yeshua anchors Him in the lineage of David, the promises of Torah, the cries of the Prophets. To redact that name is to redact the story. To rename the Redeemer is to reframe the redemption.

So we must ask: *What were they preserving?* A faith? Perhaps. A structure? Certainly. But the covenantal heartbeat of Yeshua's mission? Silenced. Renamed. Omitted.

Ignatius is a prime example of this vision of self. His theology offers us not clarity, but mystery. And mystery, for him, is the closest thing to a hermeneutical principle. We see this most clearly in his letter to the Magnesians, chapter 9. There is not one reference to the authority of Scripture. Not one. His citations serve doctrinal scaffolding, not interpretive foundation.

If Ignatius had a maxim, it would read:

> "Man does not live by the Word of the Lord, but by association with the bishop, presbyter, or deacon."

Scripture is not the source, it's the seasoning. The real authority is positional. His use of "charters" has been interpreted as structural, but I must offer two clarifications:

1. The "charter" he refers to is responsive, not prescriptive.
2. It is not hermeneutical, it is personified. Authority is embodied, not exegeted. [35]

His frequent statements regarding polity, bishop, presbyter, deacon, establish what is requisite for the faith. Though not a formal declaration of hermeneutic, he writes as if ecclesial hierarchy is the interpretive lens. The bishop is not just a leader; he is the living charter. The creed walks on two legs. He writes:

Μη πλανασθε ταις ετεροδοξιαις μηδε
μυθευμασιν τοις παλαιοις ανωφελεσιν
ουσιν.ει γαρ μεχρι νυν κατα
Ιουδαισμον ζωμεν, ομολογουμεν χαριν
μη ειληφεναι.[36]

The translation would be ; Don't be deceived by strange doctrines or by antiquated myths, which are worthless. For if from now on, we live according to Judaism, we admit that we have not received grace. His use of Ιουδαισμον , to live according to Judaism, in this case the negative sense.

The Lord's own words ring with clarity:

> *"Therefore whatever they tell you to observe, that you observe and do, but do not do according to their works; for they say, and do not do."*
> *—Matthew 23:3*

This is not ambiguity. It's a demarcation. And it draws a line, one that Ignatius stepped over with conviction. His statement:

"Ατοπον εστιν, Ιησουν Χριστον λαλειν και Ιουδαιζειν

..." "It is out of place to speak of Jesus Christ and to Judaize..." confirms the divide.

But let's be precise. What Ignatius meant by "Judaism" was not Jewish proselytizing, because they didn't practice that. The issue was not outreach. It was **practice**. The manner of life. The halachic rhythm. The Torah-shaped walk of the Messiah Himself.

Rabbinic Judaism was part of what he objected to, yes, but the deeper offense was the idea that one could follow Yeshua and still walk as He walked. That obedience to Torah was not just historical, but exemplary. That *1 John 2:6 "Whoever claims to live in Him must walk as He walked"* was not metaphor, but mandate.

This would have fallen on deaf ears across most of the Empire. And it still does. It is rejected officially by all of Christendom and Judaism today. Even the Messianic movement, for all its zeal, often stops short. Most honor the Decalogue—but they do so by keeping all eight of the commandments. The other two are theological inconveniences.

And the example of Ruth—a Gentile who said *"Your people shall be my people, and your God my God"*—seems lost. Her grafting was not symbolic. It was covenantal. She didn't just join the story; she joined the walk.

The Ante Nicene Benchmark Chart

Exactly what was their alignment with divine instruction?
To what were they shadow of?

What this chart on the "engagement" of the Ante-Nicene Fathers with Jewish understanding really reveals is that *interaction* is a misnomer. These men weren't dialoguing, they were missing the boat entirely. The so-called "Jewish understanding" they engage with is a straw man, a theological scarecrow stuffed with rabbinic caricature and polemical intent.

Let's be clear: the Jews depicted here, whether historical interlocutors or literary devices, represent rabbinic Judaism, not the covenantal lifeblood of the tribes of Israel. They function as antagonist, foil, or both, crafted to serve a rhetorical purpose. The Fathers weren't wrestling with the sacred continuity of Israel; they were staging a drama where Judaism plays the villain, so that the Church can emerge as the hero.

This isn't engagement. It's replacement theater,

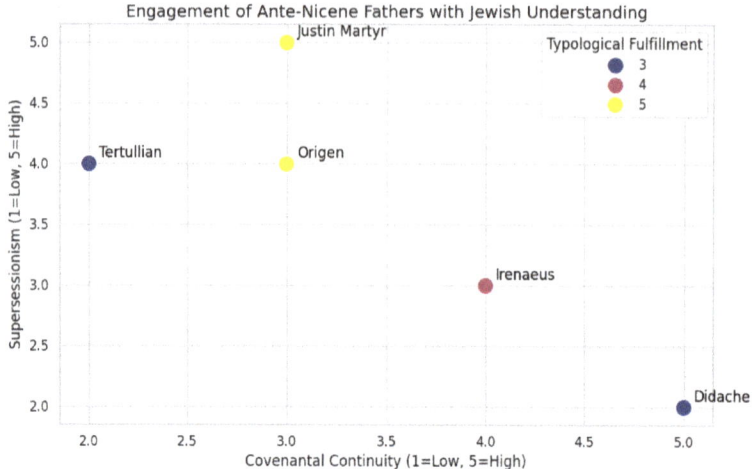

How to Read the Chart

- **X-axis**: Degree of Covenantal Continuity (1 = low, 5 = high)
- **Y-axis**: Degree of Supersessionism (1 = low, 5 = high)
- **Color Hue**: Intensity of Typological Fulfillment (darker = stronger typology)

The Jewish understanding(s) at this time are post-Yavneh, a seismic shift that redefined communal identity, halakhic authority, and interpretive frameworks, termed as Mesorah. And yet, I don't see this noted by any of the Apostolic or Ante-Nicene Fathers when addressing the so-called "Jewish" positions. It should have been a red flag, in that as the 'Jewish' calendar, so important to the Jews had already a essential feature, namely the Mishmarot was not present.

It's as if the rabbinic recalibration never happened. No recognition of the Sanhedrin's relocation, no awareness of the emerging halakhic consensus, no engagement with the lived reality of post-Temple Judaism. Instead, we get generic "Jews" frozen in time, idealized, vilified, or typologized to suit theological agendas.

This omission isn't just a historical blind spot. It's a hermeneutical failure. If you're going to polemicize against Judaism, at least acknowledge which Judaism you're targeting. Otherwise, you're shadowboxing with ghosts.

It's theological vaudeville. The curtain rises, the actors enter, and the script is missing page one.

There's something almost comical here. But it's the kind of comedy that makes prophets weep and angels raise eyebrows. The kind that begs the question: *If this is the legacy, what exactly are we inheriting?* This should be reframed as a satirical interlude "Ecclesial Comedy: A Tragedy in Three Acts"?

Ειρηναιος Λουγδουνου - Dramatis Personae

Irenaeus Bishop of Lugdunum, in Gaul, now Lyon in France, late second century.

Irenaeus' writings demand that the issue of continuity vs. discontinuity be reckoned with, not as a footnote, but as a hermeneutical fulcrum. His handling of the Word is not neutral. It leans. And what it leans toward reveals the fault lines that modern theology still dances across.

Today's theological schools Dispensationalism and Covenant Theology are proof that discontinuity is not just a concept; it's a system. A framework. A lens that determines what gets preserved and what gets discarded. But as asked prior: *How does discontinuity factor into the connection between prophecy and fulfillment?*

The answer is simple: negatively.

Discontinuity, as a principle, is an eliminating factor. It doesn't bridge gaps—it builds walls. It rules out certain possibilities by default. It severs the thread between what was spoken and what was realized. It turns prophecy into abstraction and fulfillment into reinvention.

This is a point J. Ligon Duncan III raised in his essay of Irenaeus' usage of the word *covenant*. [37] Duncan established that Irenaeus employed the term in two distinct ways, each revealing his hermeneutic. One use aligns with continuity, preserving the thread of divine intent. The other flirts with abstraction, allowing for theological drift.

And then he cites this statement from Irenaeus himself

> "He confessed to be His blood, and taught the new oblation of the new covenant; which the Church receiving from the apostles, offers to God throughout all the world, to Him who gives us as the means of subsistence the first-fruits of His own gifts in the New Testament, concerning which Malachi, among the twelve apostles, thus spoke beforehand" [38]

This is also cited by Jennings Ligon Duncan III, Ph.D. in Systematic and Historical Theology from the University of Edinburgh (1995), to expose Irenaeus' point: that in the New Testament, Gentiles have replaced the Jews as the people of God. [38] Labeling this as mere presumption doesn't cut it. It's not a slip, it's a system. To conclude, as Irenaeus did, that the use of covenantal language, even in rare fashion, is primarily based on the observation that *"early Christian self-understanding as the people of God"* [39] is not just a theological move. It's a hermeneutical hijack.

And in this, Duncan is correct. The self-understanding of the early Church became the lens through which Scripture was read, not the other way around. I would propose this is the prime source for the destruction of context. It's not just a misreading, it's a congenital defect. Irenaeus is writing his theology *into* the context, not *from* it. The result? A theological inversion that is deleterious to the very nature of Jeremiah's prophecy.

There is no sense none in which Jeremiah would have construed this revelation to be foreign in application. The covenant was not a Gentile abstraction. It was a promise to a people, a grafting into a root, not a replacement of it.

וְכָרַתִּי אֶת־בֵּית יִשְׂרָאֵל וְאֶת־בֵּית יְהוּדָה בְּרִית חֲדָשָׁה "*I will cut a new covenant with the house of Israel and the house of Judah.*"

Not with Rome. Not with Alexandria. Not with the Gentiles as a standalone entity. The covenant is **cut**, definitely not **transferred**.

So we must ask: *If the covenant was cut with Israel and Judah, what theological sleight of hand allows the Church to claim sole inheritance?* The answer lies not in the text, but in the trajectory. And that trajectory, if left unchallenged, leads to a theology that forgets its own root.

An obvious test, one that should have been applied long ago, is to ask how Jeremiah would have reacted to Irenaeus, Bishop of Lyon (125-202 CE) saying what he did. If Jeremiah had any notion of Gentile inclusion, it would have been governed by its connection to the House of Israel and the House of Judah. That's not conjecture, it's covenantal architecture. The New Covenant was not a theological abstraction; it was a cutting, a divine incision into the flesh of history, and its recipients were named.

So we must ask: *Was this "early Christian self-understanding" evident at the Council of Jerusalem in Acts 15?* Was the issue in Jerusalem Gentiles or Jews? The answer: Gentiles, and how they might be grafted in without severing the root.

When Paul asked, *"Has God cast away His people?"* the answer was emphatic: "God forbid." Would Irenaeus have responded the same way? Unlikely. His theological development, his consistent use of dispositio suggests otherwise. That term, while elegant, has become the fuel for centuries of dispute between Covenant Theology and Dispensationalism. But beneath the academic quarrels lies a deeper issue: Irenaeus did not grasp the complexity of the old covenant.

Consider Exodus 34 the renewal of the covenant through Moshe's intercession. This moment, rich with divine mercy and covenantal resilience, is nowhere considered in Irenaeus' framing of the New Covenant. And yet, it is central to the purpose of God. The covenant was not replaced—it was renewed. And that renewal echoes in Jeremiah's prophecy.

Yes, Irenaeus quoted Jeremiah 31:31–34. But did he make the same connection that Shaul/Paul did with Moshe? You might think so, especially if he can say *"Moysi litterae verba sint Christi"* [40] —that the words of Moses are the words of Christ. But quoting is not connecting. And connection is everything.

Would the preaching of Irenaeus' day have truly embodied the example of Romans 10:8?

> *"But what does it say? 'The word is near you, in your mouth and in your heart'—that is, the word of faith we are preaching."*

This is a direct quote from Deuteronomy 30:14. The word of faith the disciples were preaching was not a Pauline innovation, it was a Mosaic inheritance. The Torah was not abolished; it was activated.

So we must ask: Was Irenaeus, or any of his contemporaries, preaching the word of faith found in Deuteronomy? Did the Ante-Nicene Fathers recognize the singular message of the entirety of Scripture? That Moshe was indeed, as Luke 24:44 indicates, the one whose words must be fulfilled?

> *"These are My words which I spoke to you while I was still with you, that all things which are written about Me in the Law of Moses and the Prophets and the Psalms must be fulfilled." - NASB*

Fulfilled, not forgotten. Connected, not replaced. Grafted, not severed.

The question remains: Did they preach the Word? Or did they preach around it?

Did Ιωαννης Χρυσοστομος - John Chrysostom, a 4th-century Archbishop of Constantinople (347 -407) Homily 16 on Hebrews preach this word? He writes:

"And for this cause (he says) He is the mediator of the New Testament. What is a Mediator? A mediator is not lord of the thing of which he is mediator, but the thing belongs to one person, and the mediator is another: as for instance, the mediator of a marriage is not the bridegroom, but the one who aids him who is about to be married. So then also here: The Son became Mediator between God and us. The Father willed not to leave us this inheritance, but was angry against us, and was displeased [with us] as being estranged [from Him]; He accordingly became Mediator between us and Him, and prevailed with Him" [41]

Wow. What a concept marriage must have been in Chrysostom's day. Apparently, it wasn't enough to have a best man—you needed a sacrificial lamb. Just exactly *when* did the mediator of a marriage have to die? Was he part of the ceremony? When did this mediator proclaim " We who are about to die Salute you! Did he walk the bride down the aisle and then get fed to the lions as a closing benediction?

The comparison with the gladiatorial games is frightening. And not just because of the bloodsport imagery, it's the theology behind it. If the Son is the "mediator" in the same way a gladiator is the entertainment, then we've traded covenantal fidelity for cosmic spectacle. Cue the divine thumbs-up or thumbs-down. Maybe this explains all the arranged marriages, though this could be an argument for predestination.

To ask if there was any theological consesus in the time period has no good answer.

Four

Vulgatta

"G od is at home; it is we who have gone for a walk" - Meister Eckhart

Jerome's Preface to the Vulgate Version of the New Testament Addressed to Pope Damasus in A.D. 383

"You urge me, Damasus, to revise the Old Latin version of the New Testament, and, as it were, to sit in judgment on the copies of the Scriptures which are now in use. You would have me correct them, and bring them back to a form more in keeping with the Greek original. This is a task of no small difficulty, for there are as many opinions as there are copies. If, therefore, I am to be judged by my work, and not by prejudice, let me first say that I am not attempting anything new or rash, but only following the example of those who have gone before me.

The labor is indeed great, but the reward is greater. I am not unaware of the storm of abuse that will be stirred up against me by those who think that the Latin texts they possess are the true ones, and will call me a falsifier for daring to correct them. But I am comforted by the words of Scripture: 'Blessed are they who suffer persecution for righteousness' sake.'

I have tried to preserve the sense rather than the words, and to render the meaning faithfully rather than slavishly. I have not altered the order of the words unless the Greek required it. I have not added or omitted anything, but have translated as faithfully as possible.

Let those who wish to criticize me read the Greek, and then judge whether I have translated correctly. Let them not condemn me out of ignorance, but examine the evidence. If they find that I have erred, let them correct me; if not, let them acknowledge the truth.

I have begun with the Gospels, because they are the foundation of the New Testament. I have followed the order of Matthew, Mark, Luke, and John, and have translated them according to the best Greek manuscripts. I hope that my work will be useful to those who seek the truth, and that it will help to bring unity to the Church."*
[42]

Near the end of the fourth century, Latin Christendom was awash in gospel manuscripts, fragmented, inconsistent, and largely the product of congregational leaders copying texts for local use. These were the Vetus Latina, the Old Latin Bibles. Written in classical Latin, they were less a unified tradition than a patchwork of theological improvisation. The textual chaos demanded a reckoning.

Enter Eusebius Sophronius Hieronymus, known to us as Jerome. Commissioned by Pope Damasus I (366–384), Jerome was tasked with revising the Vetus Latina into a single, standardized work, drawing from the best Greek manuscripts available. This wasn't mere editing; it was a translational overhaul. And it came with political heat.

In 382, Jerome was forced to leave Rome under a cloud of scandal. Summoned before an episcopal court, he faced accusations of clerical misconduct. The details remain murky, but the whispers were sharp: legacy-hunting, manipulating wealthy patrons for inheritance, and sexual impropriety. Whether true or fabricated, the fallout was real. Jerome fled to Bethlehem, where scandal gave way to scholarship.

There, he did more than revise the Gospels. He took on the Tenach the Hebrew Scriptures, translating them directly from Hebrew, a move that defied the Septuagint-dominated tradition. He labeled his gospel compilation the Novum Testamentum, a phrase borrowed from Quintus Septimius Florens Tertullianus, Tertullian of Carthage (c. 155–220), who had coined it in his polemics against Marcion.

Jerome himself claimed to have translated the Novum Testamentum first, completing the work by 405, and dying in Bethlehem in September of 420. But what's truly noteworthy is the order in which he translated the manuscripts. It was reverse chronological, a sequence that inevitably raised questions of contextual coherence. Later texts shaped the interpretive lens for earlier ones, a hermeneutical inversion with theological consequences.

And then there's the LXX problem. Despite Jerome's insistence on Hebrew fidelity, he was not immune to pressure. Augustine of Hippo, ever the ecclesiastical heavyweight, leaned on Jerome to retain Septuagintal influence. The result? A hybrid text, part Hebrew, part Greek, part Latin, bearing the fingerprints of theological compromise.

Augustine wrote in Letter 71, Chapter 2, section 3 the following:

"In this letter I have further to say, that I have since heard that you have translated Job out of the original Hebrew, although in your own translation of the same prophet from the Greek tongue we had already a version of that book. In that earlier version you marked with asterisks the words found in the Hebrew but wanting in the Greek, and with obelisks the words found in the Greek but wanting in the Hebrew; and this was done with such astonishing exactness, that in some places we have every word distinguished by a separate asterisk, as a sign that these words are in the Hebrew, but not in the Greek. Now, however, in this more recent version from the Hebrew, there is not the same scrupulous fidelity as to the words; and it perplexes any thoughtful reader to understand either what was the reason for marking the asterisks in the former version with so much care that they indicate the absence from the Greek version of even the smallest grammatical particles which have not been rendered from the Hebrew, or what is the reason for so much less care having been taken in this recent version from the Hebrew to secure that these same particles be found in their own places. I would have put down here an extract or two in illustration of this criticism; but at present I have not access to the manuscript of the translation from the Hebrew. Since, however, your quick discernment anticipates and goes beyond not only what I have said, but also what I meant to say, you already understand, I think, enough to be able, by giving the reason for the plan which you have adopted, to explain what perplexes me." [43]

Jerome's legacy is monumental, but it is not unambiguous. His translation choices, especially around covenantal language, deserve scrutiny. *Foedus, testamentum, pactum,* each carries different connotations, and Jerome's selections shaped Western theology for centuries. The question is not merely what he translated, but how his choices reframed the covenantal narrative.

Jerome's Translational Arc: A Chronology of Sacred Interruption

The chronology of his work is as follows, not merely a list, but a theological breadcrumb trail, each entry a pivot in the war over meaning:

1. Novum Testamentum – *circa 382 The Latin voice of the Gospels, filtered through Greek syntax and Roman ambition.*
2. Psalterium Romanum – *circa 384 A liturgical placeholder, more Roman than Hebrew, more rhythm than revelation.*
3. Gallican Psalter – *circa 387 A revision, yes—but still tethered to the LXX, still echoing the Greek choir.*
4. Samuel and Kings – *circa 390 Here begins the Hebrew turn. A rupture. A return. A rebellion against consensus.*
5. Psalms (Hebrew-based) – *circa 392 Now the text breathes Hebrew again. The graft begins to show.*
6. Job and the Prophets – *circa 393 Suffering and sovereignty—translated not for comfort, but confrontation.*
7. I & II Esdras – *circa 394 Restoration literature. Post-exilic memory. The architecture of return.*
8. Chronicles – *circa 396 A priestly retelling. A theological mirror. A genealogy of covenant.*

Then, pause. A break in the work due to illness. The translator, once relentless, is silenced. Not by Rome, not by critics, but by the frailty of flesh. Even scribes must wrestle with mortality.

And yet

9. Proverbs, Ecclesiastes, Canticle – *circa 398 Wisdom literature, post-illness. Aphorism, irony, eros. A translator reborn.*

10. Pentateuch – *circa 401 The foundation stones. Torah rendered in Latin. Not just translation—transmission.*

11. Joshua, Judges, Ruth, Esther – *circa 405 Conquest, chaos, covenant, and courage. The narrative arc of divine fidelity.*

Jerome, like all *translatores*, had choices to make. And not just lexical ones, these were theological, political, and deeply contextual. The question of what role context played in his work is not only legitimate, it's unavoidable. Three fault lines demand attention:

First, the order of his work. Jerome did not translate canonically or chronologically. He began with the *Novum Testamentum*, then spiraled backward into the Hebrew canon. This reverse sequencing shaped interpretive flow, later texts became the lens for earlier ones. It's not just a logistical choice; it's a hermeneutical inversion.

Second, the terms he employed. Jerome's Latin was not neutral. His choices *foedus, testamentum, pactum,* were freighted with theological consequence. These weren't mere synonyms; they were doctrinal signposts. His vocabulary reframed covenant, law, and grace for the Latin Church, often in ways that obscured Hebraic nuance.

Third, the influence exerted upon him. Jerome was not translating in a vacuum. He was pressured, by ecclesiastical politics, by Augustine's insistence on Septuagintal fidelity, by the expectations of Rome. His Hebrew turn was radical, but it was also contested. The translator became a battleground.

So yes, context matters. Not as backdrop, but as battleground. Jerome's work is not just a translation; it's a theological intervention.

The Unspoken Influence on Jerome's Translational Choices

To the three fault lines, sequence, lexicon, and ecclesiastical pressure, we must add a fourth: liturgy.

Liturgy wasn't just backdrop, it was substrate. The Vetus Latina texts Jerome was revising weren't theoretical manuscripts; they were functional, embedded in the rhythm of worship. Psalms chanted, Gospels proclaimed, epistles recited—all within the living breath of congregational liturgy. These texts had devotional inertia. To revise them was to risk disrupting the sacred cadence of the Church's voice.

Jerome knew this. His early revisions, the Psalterium Romanum, the Gallican Psalter, were liturgically cautious. He didn't just translate; he negotiated. The tension between textual fidelity and liturgical familiarity shaped his choices. Even his vocabulary for covenant *testamentum* over *foedus* was not merely theological; it was auditory, chosen for how it would sound in the mouth of the priest and the ear of the laity.

And then there's the pressure from Augustine, who insisted that Jerome's Hebrew turn not fracture the liturgical unity of the Latin Church. The Septuagint, for Augustine, was not just a translation, it was tradition, sanctified by usage. Jerome's resistance was bold, but not absolute. His final product bears the marks of compromise.

So yes, liturgy was the fourth influence. Not as a theological argument, but as a rhythmic constraint. Jerome translated with one eye on the manuscript, and the other on the sanctuary.

The Ratios That Betray the Rhythm

Evidence of this fracture is numerical, not merely lexical. In the Vulgate, Jerome's rendering of *Brit* breaks down as follows: *foedus* at 54.9%, *pactum* at 40%, and *testamentum* limping in at a paltry 3%. These aren't just translation choices, they're theological evasions. The ratios themselves confess what the text cannot: that the prophetic arc, from utterance to incarnation, is unmapped. There is no semantic tether between the covenant announced and the covenant fulfilled.

It should follow, logically, liturgically, covenantally, that a term used in prophecy would echo in its fulfillment. That the voice of Isaiah would reverberate in the mouth of Paul. But this is not the case. The thread is cut. The fulfillment arrives wearing a different name, as if the bridegroom forgot the bride's language.

Why? Because Jerome did not see it. Not because he lacked skill, but because the goal was reached prior to its antecedent. He translated backwards, from ecclesial endpoint to textual origin, retrojecting doctrinal conclusions into linguistic decisions. The covenant was already "fulfilled," so the prophetic was treated as prelude, not promise. The result? A semantic dismembering of sacred continuity. Just how a *prophesied covenant* morphed into a *testament* as its fulfillment is the point. Not a footnote. Not a semantic shrug. It is the theological sleight of hand that rebranded continuity as closure. The covenant, spoken in promise, was fulfilled in a term foreign to its own vocabulary *testamentum*, a juridical relic with no prophetic ancestry. This is not fulfillment; it is substitution masquerading as completion.

There is proof of this. Jerome's own prologue to Jeremiah belays it, when he refers to the prophet as *"a man of the Gospel to the Church."[44]* That phrase is not innocent. It is a hermeneutical override, a retroactive grafting of ecclesial identity onto a covenantal messenger. Jeremiah, whose voice thundered within the framework of *Brit*, is rebranded as a proto-Christian emissary. The covenantal context is collapsed into a liturgical endpoint. The prophet is no longer speaking to Israel, but to a Church that did not yet exist.

This is not translation, it is transposition. The fulfillment is assumed, and the antecedent is rewritten to match. The covenant becomes *testament*, the prophet becomes evangelist, and the continuity is severed in the name of doctrinal symmetry. Jerome did not merely translate Jeremiah—he repurposed him.

Jerome's Treatment of Jeremiah 31:31 — *"From the Original Greek"*?

Ecce dies veniunt dicit Dominus et feriam domui Israhel et domui Iuda foedus novum.

This is Jerome's Latin rendering of Jeremiah 31:31. And it demands scrutiny—not just for what it says, but for what it assumes.

Let's begin with the verb: feriam. From *ferio*, meaning *to strike, smite, beat, knock, cut, or thrust*. A violent term. A term of rupture. And yet here it is, yoked to foedus, a neuter singular noun meaning *league, compact, treaty*. The covenant is not *given*, *established*, or *renewed*, it is struck. As if the divine act were a blow, not a bond.

And what of foedus itself? It's not *testamentum*, not *pactum*, but *foedus*, a term with Roman juridical overtones, more suited to treaties between warring states than to the sacred continuity of *Brit*. It's clinical. Contractual. Devoid of liturgical warmth or prophetic resonance.

So we must ask: is there any hermeneutics involved here? Or is this translation a theological retrofit, an attempt to align Hebrew prophecy with Latin categories, smoothing the jagged edges of covenantal fidelity into the polished marble of ecclesial doctrine?

Jerome claims to translate "from the original Greek." But Jeremiah 31:31 is Hebrew, not Greek. The Septuagint's rendering is already a layer removed. So what Jerome offers is not a return to the fountainhead, but a triangulated echo, Hebrew to Greek to Latin, each step introducing semantic drift.

The result? A covenant that is struck, not cut. A promise rendered as a treaty. A prophetic utterance reframed as a juridical act. The hermeneutics here are not exegesis, they are ecclesial choreography, designed to make the text dance to Rome's rhythm.

Testamentum Disponam vs. Foedus Feriam:

Jeremiah 31:31 → Hebrews 8:8 Jeremiah 31:33 → Hebrews 8:10

Let us begin not with ecclesial euphemism, but with prophetic incision.

Jeremiah 31:31 — *Ecce dies veniunt, dicit Dominus, et feriam domui Israel et domui Iuda foedus novum.*

The Vulgate's rendering here is surgical: *feriam foedus.* The verb *feriam* (from *ferio*) is not gentle, it is violent. To strike, to smite, to cut. The covenant is not whispered, it is hammered into history. And the noun *foedus,* a neuter singular term for treaty or compact, evokes Roman legalism, not Hebraic intimacy. This is covenant as rupture, not relationship.

But when the same prophetic utterance is quoted in Hebrews 8:8, the Latin shifts. And the shift is not cosmetic, it is theological.

Hebrews 8:8 — *Ecce dies veniunt, dicit Dominus, et consummabo super domum Israel et super domum Iuda testamentum novum.*

Now the covenant is no longer *foedus,* it is *testamentum.* And the verb is no longer *feriam,* it is *consummabo.* The violence is gone. The covenant is not struck, it is fulfilled. *Testamentum* carries the weight of inheritance, legacy, and death. It is not a treaty, it is a will. And *consummabo* (from *consummare*) means to complete, to perfect, to bring to its telos.

This is not a lexical accident. It is a hermeneutical recalibration. The preacher of Hebrews reframes the prophetic incision as a Christological consummation. The covenant is no longer a new wound, it is the healing of an old one. The Latin betrays the theological pivot: from rupture to resolution, from treaty to testament.

Jeremiah 31:33 — *Dabo legem meam in visceribus eorum, et in corde eorum scribam eam.*

Here, the covenant moves inward. The law is not merely given, it is implanted. *Viscera,* the guts, the innermost parts. *Cor,* the heart. And the verb: *scribam* I will write. This is divine inscription, not proclamation. The covenant is not external, it is embodied.

This is not Rome's *testamentum*, it is Israel's internal Torah.

Hebrews 8:10 — *Dabo leges meas in mentem eorum, et in corde eorum scribam eas: et ero eis in Deum, et ipsi erunt mihi in populum.*

Again, the preacher preserves *scribam*, the act of writing, but shifts *viscera* to *mentem*, the mind. The covenant moves from gut to cognition, from visceral to intellectual. The heart remains, but the center of gravity shifts. This is not betrayal, it is reframing. The law is still internal, but now it is understood, not merely felt.

And here, the Latin introduces another verb: *disponam*. In some manuscripts and commentaries, *disponam testamentum* appears "I will arrange a testament." From *disponere*: to set in order, to arrange, to establish. This is covenant as administration, not confrontation. The divine act becomes a legal structuring, a heavenly estate plan.

Comparative Lexical Table: Latin Covenant Terminology

Verse	Covenant Term	Qualifier Verb	Semantic Tone	Theological Implication
Jeremiah 31:31	*foedus novum*	*feriam*	Violent, juridical	Covenant as rupture
Hebrews 8:8	*testamentum novum*	*consummabo*	Fulfilled, telic	Covenant as completion
Hebrews (alt.)	*testamentum novum*	*disponam*	Administrative	Covenant as structured legacy
Jeremiah 31:33	—	*scribam*	Embodied, visceral	Law inscribed in the body
Hebrews 8:10	—	*scribam*	Cognitive, internal	Law inscribed in the mind

Is this a puzzle, a quiz, to see how many meanings you can find?

Testamentum ad Nauseam

Sacerdotalism and the Testamentum Trap

The next, no, the compounding, issue arises from the sacerdotal scaffolding erected atop his epistolary architecture. What began as a linguistic shift metastasized into sacramental reengineering. The covenant, once a visceral bond between YHWH and Israel, blood-bound, land-anchored, possession-driven, was now filtered through the juridical lens of *testamentum,* a Latin calque that smuggled in Roman inheritance law under the guise of theological continuity. From there, the covenant ossified into the ecclesial machinery of priesthood and sacrament: a systematized liturgy of intermediaries, rites, and semantic drift. This was not development. It was transmutation, a fundamental alteration of the covenanted's nature. A shift that occurs at least 105 times in the KJV. The shift was not merely architectural; it was ontological. And the evidence? It lingers in the lexicon. Inheritance has replaced possession. The former is passive, posthumous, juridical. The latter is active, immediate, covenantal. Inheritance follows naturally from testamentum, a will, a death, a legal transfer. But *possession* belongs to covenant, living, present, enacted. Yet in English translations, possession is conspicuously absent. It is never used. Not once. The semantic scaffolding has done its work. The meaning has been changed. Scripturally speaking, possession is not shuffled by parchment, it is transferred by touch. The laying on of hands is the mechanism, not the metaphor. It is termed the pronouncement of a measure of blessing, not a sentimental gesture. This act, seen roughly 25 to 30 times in the biblical corpus, is the architecture of authorization. It marks separation, appointment, and covenantal flow. Jacob blessing Ephraim and Manasseh (Genesis 48:14–20) is a prominent example of this and it is called Blessing, not inheritance. The hand is not ornamental. It is the typographic conduit by which stewardship is conferred.

What's critical, what any catechumen of the late classical period would have understood intuitively, is that *testamentum* was not a synonym for *foedus*. It was a legal instrument of death, not a living bond of fidelity. George Long, M.A., Fellow of Trinity College, addresses this with surgical clarity in his article found in *A Dictionary of Greek and Roman Antiquities* (William Smith, John Murray, London, 1875). [45]

Let us extract a few specifics:

> *Testamentum* is defined as *"mentis nostrae justa contestatio in id solemniter facta ut post mortem nostram valeat."* Translation: "A just declaration of our will, solemnly made so that it may be valid after our death."

This is not covenantal continuity, it is posthumous delegation. The testator must possess *testamentifactio,* the legal capacity to make a valid will. And who had this capacity?

> *Testamentifactio* was the privilege only of Roman citizens who were *patresfamilias.*

So the "new covenant," reframed as *testamentum,* was not merely a theological innovation, it was a juridical colonization. The covenant was no longer a shared vow, it became a unilateral bequest, valid only upon death, and accessible only to those with Roman legal standing.

This is the architecture upon which sacerdotalism was built:

- A *testamentum* requires a death.
- A death requires a priesthood to administer its effects.
- And thus, the living covenant was buried beneath the weight of Roman legalism and ecclesial mediation.

The irony? The very term that was meant to signal divine intimacy *testamentum* was, in its classical usage, a mechanism of exclusion, reserved for Roman patriarchs.

Testamentum were formed by one of three modes:
a. at Calata Comitia
b. Testamentum in procinctu
c. Testamentum per aes et libruam

From Berit to Bureaucracy: The Testamentum Misfire

The formal aspects of Roman *testamentum* were not spiritual, they were *jure facta*, acts of law. The Twelve Tables, that early monument to civic codification, recognized a man's sovereign power to dispose of his property as he pleased. The Latin reads:

> *Uti legassit super pecunia tutelave suae rei ita jus esto.* - As he shall have declared concerning his property or guardianship, so let it be law.

This was not covenantal fidelity, it was juridical finality. And the ritual was theatrically Roman. The testator, grasping the wax tablets, would pronounce:

> *Haec ita ut in his tabulis cerisque (or cerisve) scripta sunt ita do ita lego ita testor itaque vos Quirites testimonium mihi perhibetote.* "As these things are written in these tablets and wax, so I give, so I bequeath, so I testify—and you, O Quirites, bear witness for me."

This was the *nuncupatio*, the public publishing of the will. A performative seal. A civic liturgy of legal closure.

And it was never spoken by Yeshua. Nor could it have been. He was not a Roman citizen. He did not possess *testamentifactio*, the legal standing to make a valid will under Roman law. His words were covenantal, not codicillary.

The Witness Clause That Would Have Silenced James

But the absurdity deepens. Roman law forbade family members from serving as witnesses in a *testamentum*. Why? Because the *familiae emtio*, the symbolic sale of the estate, was supposed to be a real transaction. And real transactions required disinterested parties. Anyone under the *potestas* of the *familiae emtor* or the *testator* was disqualified.

This would have disqualified Yaakov (James), the brother of Yeshua, from bearing witness. Had the New Testament been structured as a Roman *testamentum*, James's epistle would have been legally inadmissible. His familial proximity would have nullified his testimony.

So let us be clear: the institutional scaffolding of *testamentum*, its civic rites, legal exclusions, and performative declarations, has **nothing to do** with the historical Near Eastern *berit*, nor with the biblical covenantal context.

The Fifth-Century Shift: From Covenant to Codicil

By the early fifth century, we witness a theological transmutation. The sacred בְּרִית the bond of mutual fidelity, s replaced by *testamentum*, a posthumous declaration administered by ecclesial scribes and validated by imperial law.

And what is lost?

Jeremiah 31:31. *"I will put My Torah..."* The direct object marker אֶת binds *My Torah* into the covenantal structure. It is not an addendum, it is the **content** of the covenant. But under the logic of *testamentum*, this is stricken from consideration. The Torah becomes a relic, not a relational bond. The *covenants of promise* are gutted of their textual heart.

Covenant or Codicil? The Legal Foundations of Kingdom and the Vulgate's Drift

The initial and contextual parallel of covenant in the Ancient Near East is, undeniably, a legal issue. This is not incidental, it is foundational. For what is a kingdom without law? Whether we speak of the Kingdom of God, the Kingdom of Israel, or the Davidic Throne to which Messiah is irrevocably tethered, we are not dealing with an amorphous spiritual abstraction. We are dealing with juridical content, terms, stipulations, obligations, and fidelity.

The LORD is not instituting a mystical fog. He is establishing a kingdom with legal architecture, and the covenant is its constitutional backbone.

So we must ask: was this legal clarity preserved as the Church entered the Middle Ages, armed with the Vulgate and its Latin categories? This was the era in which Greek and Latin were prominent, but Hebrew was marginalized. And with that marginalization came a semantic drift, from *berit* to *testamentum*, from mutual fidelity to unilateral declaration.

This proposition has been challenged with precision by Daniel Gruber. His concerns over the translation and interpretation of Hebrews 9:15–18 are not speculative—they are contextually undeniable. He writes:

> *"The first concerns the phrase 'the mediator of a new testament.' No such thing exists. A testament, on the other hand, is the declaration of one individual. There is no mediator involved in the solitary issuance of a testament. There can only be a mediator when there are two or more parties involved."*[46]

This is not a minor quibble, it is a hermeneutical fault line. The Vulgate's framing of *testamentum* as the fulfillment of *berit* introduces a legal fiction. A testament requires no negotiation, no mutuality, no mediator. It is a unilateral posthumous declaration, valid only upon death. But a covenant, especially in the ANE context, is a bilateral agreement, often ratified with blood, but always requiring two parties and a mediator to broker the terms.

So when Hebrews speaks of Messiah as *mediator of a new covenant*, the Latin rendering *testamentum* collapses the very logic of mediation. It reframes the covenant as a will, and the Messiah as its executor, not its broker.

This has been the problem ever since the late classical period. The semantic shift from *berit* to *testamentum* did not clarify—it obscured. It replaced covenantal continuity with juridical finality. And the result was a theological architecture that excluded Israel, erased mutuality, and institutionalized unilateralism.

I do highly recommend Gruber's book. His conclusions are not just compelling, they are lexically and contextually inescapable.

Is this a true evaluation of Jerome, or merely the result of his work?

The answer lies not in Jerome's intent, but in the effects that echoed through the Middle Ages. It is one thing to translate; it is another to reframe reality. Jerome may have labored with sincerity, but the Vulgate's lexical architecture became a theological scaffolding that shaped, and in many cases, distorted, the Western Church's understanding of covenant, law, and kingdom.

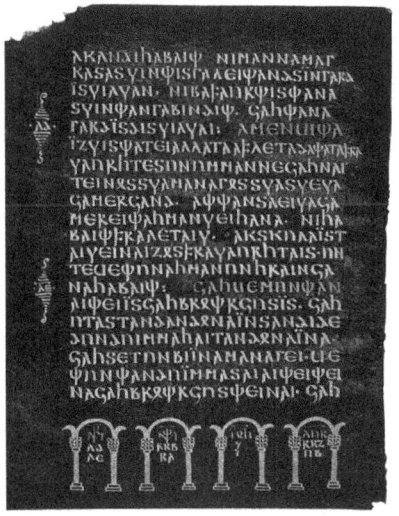

Meanwhile in the north of the Empire Bishop Ulfilas (Wulfila) c. 311 - c. 382 completed a translation as well as the creation of an alphabet for the eastern Germanic tribes. The Gothic tongue was open to the translation of the Greek texts. Now regarding the topic of covenant the issue as to whether a dispute existed between Auxentius Durostrorum and Paul Ellington over the inclusion of Hebrews, becomes relevant is its omission in the Argenteus, Ambrosianus A-E, Carolinus, Gissensis or the Fragmenta Pannonica. This would render any conclusive statements about the transmission of the cognate for covenant impossible. What could be the only addressable is the pericopes, some 40 morphological occurance of the Lemma 'triggws'. As a noun or adjective or adverb, it represents the cognates for the Greek πιστος, διαθηκης, and πεπεισμενος. These are found in the following verses where he wrote: I will provide the Latin transliterations:

Source for these is https://www.stepbible.org/version.jsp?version=Wulfila

Luke 1:72 taujan armahairtipa bi attam unsaraim jah gamunan <u>triggwos</u> weihaizos seinaizos

II Corinthians 3:6 izei jah wairþans brahta uns andbahtans niujaizos <u>triggwos</u>, ni bokos, ak ahmins; unte boka usquimith, ith ahma gauiujith.

Colossians 4:7 Þatei bi mik ist, all gakanneiþ izwis twkeikus, sa liuba broþar jah <u>triggwva</u> andbahts jah gaskalki in fraujin; þatei bi mik ist, all gakanneiþ izwis twkekus, sa liuba broþar jah triggwva andbahts jah gaskalki in fraujin.

I Timothy 4:9 <u>Triggw</u> þata waurd jah allaizos andanumtais wairþ

Philippians 1:25 Jah þata <u>triggwaba</u> wait þatei wisa jah þairhfwisa at allaim izwis du izwaraim framgahtai jah fahedai galaubeinai izwarizaiz.

It may well have been transmitted correctly, if the preceding verses are read not as isolated liturgical fragments but in deliberate connection with his rendering of *I Corinthians 11:25*: Swah samaleiko jah stikl afar nahtamata quithands: sa stikls so niujō <u>triggw</u> ist in meinamma bloþa; þata waurkjaith, swa ufta swe drigkaith, du meinai gamundai.

This is no mere formulaic repetition. It is a covenantal refrain, one that, if heard rightly, reframes the entire passage as a polemic against supersessionist readings. The phrase "niujō triggw" does not announce replacement; it anchors continuity. It is not a rupture but a reaffirmation, not a new invention but a renewed fidelity. The blood is not abstract, it is meinamma bloþa, personal, covenantal, and irrevocably Jewish.

And if one were to trace bloþa across Gothic, Greek, and Hebrew sacrificial lexicons, the irony deepens. The very medium of supposed discontinuity, blood, is the seal of continuity. The covenant is not discarded; it is ratified. The "new" is not novel, it is faithful.

As for his name Wulfila, "little wolf" perhaps it is fitting. A creature of cunning, navigating imperial terrain with apostolic teeth. Not devouring the flock, but guarding the remnant. Not replacing the root, but grafting with precision.

Say the word, and I'll build the visual theology chart. Color-coded, cross-linguistic, and unapologetically covenantal.

Five

Middle Ages - A Mid-Life Crisis?

'Speak English!' said the Eaglet. 'I don't know the meaning of half those long words, and, what's more, I don't believe you do either!' And the Eaglet bent down its head to hide a smile: some of the other birds tittered audibly. - Alice in Wonderland, chapter III

There were many authors who emerged in the next great turning of Europe's life, a period not defined by the people who lived it, but by the historians who later carved it into epochs. These time-slices, Early, High, Late, are not divine appointments but interpretive scaffolds, a heuristic architecture gifted to us by Petrarch's lament and Baronius's Latin grief. Their model, though artificial, remains useful: it marks the transition from the Classical to the so-called Dark, and into the Early Middle Ages. But just as the ages shifted, so too did the understanding of the people within them, politically, theologically, existentially.

The crises of this era are not few. They are legion. Famine, plague, fragmentation, theological rupture, the sheer density of upheaval staggers the imagination. And yet, amid the disarray, certain authors wrote with a clarity that betrays their situational awareness. They were not merely chroniclers of collapse; they were interpreters of meaning. They understood the worldview they inhabited, and they wrote as if their words might anchor it.

This chapter will concern itself with them, not merely with their names, but with their treatises, their manuscripts, their rhetorical posture. These texts are not relics. They are mirrors. And in them we will search not only for what these authors said, but for how they saw themselves, and what that self-perception reveals about the theological architecture of their age. I will narrow the lens to eight individuals, not merely for their notoriety, but for the literary gravity they carry within the theological and cultural fault lines of their age. Each is tethered to a body of work that does more than reflect its time; it refracts it. Their treatises, commentaries, and polemics will serve as the primary terrain of this chapter, not as static texts, but as living arguments. It is through these manuscripts that their worldview, their situational awareness, and their interpretive posture will be interrogated. The first of which is so self-evident, so gravitational in historical magnitude, that to omit him would border on intellectual malpractice. His presence is not optional, it is foundational. To exclude him would not merely be an oversight; it would call into question one's historical judgment altogether. He is a fixed point in the interpretive constellation, and any serious treatment of this period must begin with his orbit.

1.   Gregory the Great (540–604): The Promissio Paradigm

Merovingian
ligatures

To speak of Gregory without invoking covenant is to miss the marrow of his theological architecture. The man who straddled the ruins of empire and the rise of Christendom did not merely inherit Latin, he weaponized it for pastoral precision.

It has been proposed, rightly, if one has eyes to see, that Gregory's long-forgotten *Letania Septiformis* marked the hinge between worlds: the last breath of the classical Roman papacy and the first gasp of the medieval ecclesial order. Seven processions, seven social strata, sevenfold supplication, this was no mere liturgical flourish. It was a theological cartography of a city in crisis, a choreography of repentance that re-scripted Rome from imperial relic to sacred prototype.

In 590, Gregory did not simply respond to plague, famine, and political fragmentation with pious theatrics. He reimagined the city as a living icon, a penitential body whose limbs converged on mercy. The angel atop Hadrian's Mausoleum was not just a miracle, it was a metaphor. The sword sheathed was not only the end of pestilence, but the beginning of a thousand-year ecclesiology: hierarchical, penitential, and eschatologically charged.

This was not nostalgia. It was inauguration. Gregory's Rome did not bury the classical past, it transfigured it. And in doing so, it laid the groundwork for a society that would chant its way through centuries of plague, schism, and reform, always tracing the steps of that sevenfold litany.

Among the seven covenant-bearing terms *foedus, pactum, testamentum, promissio, dispensatio, mysterium,* and *sacramentum* Gregory's favored blade was *promissio*. Not by accident, but by design.

Gregory never associates the *mediator* with his employment of covenant. Across seventeen occurrences of the term, the referent is ontological, not contractual. There is no ratification language, no juridical sealing, only metaphysical positioning. The *mediator between God and man* is not a covenantal officiant but a theological variation, a Christological axis around which Gregory's Trinitarian clarity turns.

Take his formulation:

" Since, then, a mediator is not a mediator of one, And God is one, not divided among the Persons in Whom we have been taught to believe (for the Godhead in the Father, the Son, and the Holy Ghost is one), the Lord, therefore, becomes a mediator once for all betwixt God and men, binding man to the Deity by Himself." [47]

This is not covenantal ratification, it is ontological fusion. The binding is not by oath or sacrificial blood, but by divine nature. Gregory's *mediator* is not the executor of a promissio; he is the embodiment of divine unity. The covenant, when it appears, is pastoral and promissory. The mediator, when invoked, is metaphysical and incarnational.

To conflate the two is to miss Gregory's theological architecture. He is not a covenantal courtroom; he is sketching a metaphysical bridge. And that distinction matters. It is the difference between a treaty and a theophany. His statement-

'For this cause the mediator between God and man having assumed the first-fruits of all human nature' [48]

All of Gregory's writings, whether pastoral, polemical, or penitential, sing in harmony with his self-designation as *servus servorum Dei.* He was no imperial pontiff cloaked in triumphalism, but a shepherd who saw himself as the lowest rung in the ecclesial ladder, the hinge between divine mercy and human frailty. His letters, homilies, and *Moralia* all bear the mark of this humility: a man who trembled before the weight of souls entrusted to him.

Except, of course, when he starts whispering to animals.

There, the tone shifts. The theological rigor softens into something almost folkloric, holy Dr. Dolittle with a cassock. Doves, dogs, and serpents become allegorical playthings, vessels of divine mystery or moral instruction. It's charming, yes, but also jarringly tender. One wonders if the *servus servorum Dei* occasionally longed to be *amicus animalium Dei,* the friend of God's creatures, just for a moment.

Still, even in his zoological musings, Gregory's humility bleeds through. He doesn't dominate the beasts; he listens to them. And perhaps that, too, is service. Perhaps the whisper is just another form of prayer.

2. **Benedict of Nursai** (480-543) and the Benedictine Order.

This order, early, earnest, and reformist, was no mere accident of ascetic enthusiasm. It was the institutional echo of the *Regula Magistri,* filtered through the contemplative rigor of John Cassian. What began as a call to piety, a yearning for purity in the wilderness of post-imperial collapse, inevitably calcified into polity. And with polity came the perennial temptation: to mistake structure for sanctity, rhythm for righteousness, and communal silence for divine speech.

Castor of Apt, bless him, sought something more tender, an ecclesiola of affections, not just afflictions. But affection cannot be legislated. Unitio and Theosis[49] cannot be scheduled. And morality, does not yield to monastic architecture. The

Rule[50], though voluntary, became a scaffold for status, not a ladder to heaven. It was pedagogy masquerading as soteriology.

Let us be clear: the prologue and its 73 chapters were never meant to be exhaustive. But that's precisely the problem. To claim *passionibus Christi per patientiam participemur, ut et regno eius mereamur esse consortes*[51], that through suffering we merit the Kingdom, within a monastic framework, is to stretch the Pauline arc beyond its tensile strength. Scripture does not endorse a cloistered Kingdom. It proclaims a covenantal one.

And therein lies the great omission. The Benedictine Rule and its progeny, Cluniacs, Cistercians, Carmelites, did not fail because they lacked discipline. They failed because they lacked διαθήκη. No covenantal foundation. No mediatorial architecture. No διαθησομαι in the office of a conciliator. The very word *mediator* is conspicuously absent.

What they offered was not mediation but modulation. A social statement, not a sacramental one. They could teach, yes. They could model, yes. But they could not atone. They could not reconcile. They could not covenant. And in that absence, the Kingdom remained distant, structured, silent, and unmediated.

3.

Cassiodorus (c48-585)

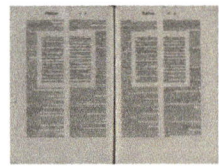

To him is accredited the *Glossa Ordinaria*, though the attribution is more tradition than testimony, more echo than evidence. The name clings to figures like Walafrid Strabo or Anselm of Laon, but the textual sediment tells a more complex story: a slow accretion of marginalia, commentary, and scholastic formatting that resists singular authorship. It is, in essence, a medieval palimpsest.

The *Glossa* itself is a marvel of pedagogical architecture. Its layout mimics the Talmud, not in theology, but in topology. Scripture sits at the center, surrounded by glosses like sentinels, guarding meaning, guiding interpretation, and occasionally smuggling in polemic. It became the standard apparatus for instruction from the Carolingian period onward, a kind of exegetical infrastructure that shaped the minds of clerics and canonists alike. This is not mere commentary. It is catechesis by collage. The *Glossa Ordinaria* does not explain Scripture, it encircles it, interrogates it, and occasionally weaponizes it. It is the medieval mind in motion: reverent, recursive, and rhetorically armed.

4.   **Isidore of Seville (560-636)**
Isidore's Lexicon of Absence: A Polemical Reading of *Etymologiae*
His extensive work *Etymologiae* serves as nothing short of a compendium of and for his time. It is not merely a dictionary, but a cultural scaffolding: a lexical ark built to preserve Roman-Christian civilization from the floodwaters of barbarism and doctrinal drift. Many of his contemporaries, and those who followed, acknowledged him as authoritative. That is not to say they agreed in all things, only that they recognized the architecture of his thought as foundational, even when the mortar crumbled under theological scrutiny.

He presided over the Fourth Council of Toledo and the Synod of Seville, not as a prophet but as a magistrate. His writings do not breathe, they legislate. They set out to establish or reflect the conventions of laws and times, not the ruptures of covenantal renewal. The structure of the *Etymologiae* makes this clear: it is ordered, exhaustive, and institutionally inclined. But it is precisely this structure that betrays its theological anemia.

His lexical omissions are not incidental. The absence of *mediator*, *conciliator*, *intercessor*, *prector*, *sequestrum* terms that would have allowed him to engage the Hebraic grammar of Messiah, renders him mute on the very axis of redemption. He cannot speak of the One who stands between, who reconciles, who bears the covenantal tension in His own body. The silence is deafening.

Nor does he employ the Latin equivalents for διαθήκη or διαθήσομαι, the covenantal verbs and nouns that thunder through Jeremiah 31 and Hebrews 8. Yes, he uses *testamentum* and *foedus*, but these are deployed in juridical or historical registers, not prophetic ones. They are abstractions, not incarnations. They are Roman, not Hebraic.

He makes no reference to the thirty-first chapter of Jeremiah, where the New Covenant is not merely declared but inscribed. Nor to Hebrews 8, where the covenantal shift is not just theological but priestly. The closest he comes is a citation of Hebrews 9:17, which he tabulates with his remark:

> *Tabulae testamenti ideo appellatae sunt, quia ante chartae et membranarum usum in dolatis tabulis non solum testamenta, sed etiam epistolarum alloquia scribebantur: unde et portitores earum tabellarii vocabantur.*[52]

Here, the "tabulae" are not Sinai's stone, but Rome's ledger. The Law is not thundered from the mountain, but etched in bureaucratic wood. That Roman legal precepts were foundational as equivalents to Biblical understandings was, sadly, a consensus of his time, and has been since. The reference to law as codified by the use of the term *tabulae* is a direct invocation of Roman jurisprudence, not prophetic covenant.

He uses this term from the beginning of Book V, with the employment of *tabulis exposuerunt*.[53] This we are to understand from him in the use of *testamentum* as found, to a large extent, in Book V—*The Book of Laws and Times*, Chapter 24, as follows: with English Translation

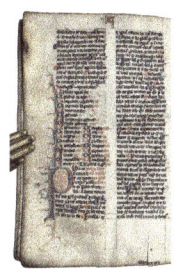

XXIV. DE INSTRVMENTIS LEGAL-IBVS. [1] Voluntas generale nomen omnium legalium instrumentorum; quae quia non vi, sed voluntate procedit, ideo tale nomen accepit. [2] Testamentum vocatum quia, nisi testator mortuus fuerit, nec confirmari potest nec sciri quid in eo scriptum sit, quia clausum et obsignatum est; et inde dictum testamentum, quia non valet nisi post testatoris monumentum, unde et Apostolus (Hebr. 9,17), 'Testamentum,' inquit, 'in mortuis confirmatur.' [3] Testamentum sane in Scripturis sanctis non hoc solum dicitur, quod non valet nisi testatoribus mortuis, sed omne pactum et placitum testamentum vocabant. Nam Laban et Iacob testamentum fecerunt, quod utique etiam inter vivos valeret, et in Psalmis legitur (82,6): 'Adversum te testamentum disposuerunt,' hoc est, pactum; et innumerabilia talia. [4] Tabulae testamenti ideo appellatae sunt, quia ante chartae et membranarum usum in dolatis tabulis non solum testamenta, sed etiam epistolarum alloquia scribebantur; unde et portitores earum tabellarii vocabantur. [5] Testamentum iuris civilis est quinque testium subscriptione firmatum. [6] Testamentum iuris praetorii est septem testium signis signatum: sed illud apud cives fit, inde civile; istud apud praetores, inde iuris praetorii. Testamentum autem signare notare est, id est ut notum sit quod scriptum est.[54]

The English : XXIV. ON LEGAL INSTRUMENTS. [1] Will is the general name of all legal instruments; which, because it proceeds not by force but by will, therefore received such a name. [2] It is called a testament because, unless the testator is dead, it cannot be confirmed nor can it be known what is written in it, because it is closed and sealed; and hence it is called a testament because it is not valid except after the memorial of the testator, whence also the Apostle (Heb. 9:17), 'A testament,' says he, 'is confirmed in the dead.' [3] In the Holy Scriptures, a testament is not only said to be valid only for dead testators, but they called every agreement and consent a testament. For Laban and Jacob made a testament, which of course was also valid between the living, and it is read in the Psalms (82:6): 'They have prepared a testament against you,' that is, a pact; and innumerable such things. [4] The tablets of the testament were so called because, before the use of paper and parchment, not only testaments but also epistles were written on carved tablets; hence the bearers of them were called postmen. [5] A testament of civil law is confirmed by the signature of five witnesses. [6] A testament of praetorian law is sealed with the signs of seven witnesses: but the former is made among citizens, hence civil; the latter among praetors, hence praetorian law. But to sign a testament is to note, that is, to make known what is written.

For which ISIDORI HISPALENSIS EPISCOPI ETYMOLOGIARUM SIVE ORIGINUM LIBER VIII **DE ECCLESIA ET SECTIS**

IV. DE HAERESIBVS IVDAEORVM. [1] Iudaei confessores interpretantur. Multos enim ex his sequitur confessio, quos antea perfidia possidebat. [2] Hebraei transitores dicuntur. Quo nomine admonentur ut de peioribus ad meliora transeant, et pristinos errores relinquant. ------

ISIDOR OF THE BISHOP OF HISTORY, ETYMOLOGIES OR ORIGIN, BOOK VIII ON THE CHURCH AND SECTS IV. ON HERESITES IVDAEORVM. [1] The Jews are interpreted as confessors. For confession follows many of them, whom perfidy had previously possessed. [2] The Hebrews are called transitors. By which name they are admonished to pass from worse to better, and to abandon their former errors.

It is clear, painfully clear, that he was anchoring his grammatical understanding in the role of *testator*, not *Mediator*. The syntax doesn't merely lean that way; it plants a flag. He wasn't fumbling through semantic ambiguity or toggling between covenantal roles. He was asserting, with linguistic precision, that the one who dies to enact the testament is the interpretive key—not the one who mediates between

parties. And that distinction isn't incidental. It's theological dyna-
mite.

5.   The Venerable Bede (673-735)

—What Bede gave to us, and to his contemporaries, is not a muddled theology of
covenant, but a lexical witness: *dedi* and *tradidit*. These are not synonyms. They are theological instruments. *Dedi* "I have given you"
is covenantal commissioning. *Tradidit* "he
handed over" is ecclesial entrustment. And the
distinction matters.

The two uses of *foedus* in Book III are strik-
ing not only for their rarity but for their isolation. They are not tethered to his two uses of *mediator*, nor do they orbit the six instances of
testamentum. This is not oversight, it is intentional architecture. Bede
is not conflating *foedus* with *testamentum*; he is letting *foedus* stand in
its own semantic gravity. His Ecclesiastical History of England gave us
the following.

He writes: *Dedi te in foedus populi, ut suscitares terram, et possideres
hereditates dissipatas, et diceres his, qui uincti sunt...* Translation: *"I have
given thee for a covenant of the people, to establish the earth, and possess the
scattered heritages; that thou mayest say to the prisoners..."-Isaiah 49:8–9*
[55]

And immediately after, he writes: *vel novi testamenti sacramenta in
commemorationem suae passionis ecclesiae celebranda tradidit* Translation:
*"Or the sacraments of the New Testament, to be celebrated by the Church in
memory of his passion, he handed over."* [56]

Notice: *foedus* is given. *Sacramenta* are handed over. The covenant is
bestowed as vocation; the sacraments are entrusted as liturgy. One is
prophetic, the other priestly. One is rooted in Isaiah's commissioning,

the other in ecclesial remembrance. To collapse them into a single semantic field is to flatten the topography of sacred meaning.

Bede knew the difference. And he preserved it, not by polemic, but
by precision.

6. John of Damascus (c. 675 - c. 749) John stands as a bridge figure,
his Greek synthesis of patristic theology and Aristotelian logic became foundational for Latin scholasticism, but he himself remained
firmly within the Greek monastic and liturgical tradition. His absence
from Latin authorship is part of what makes his later adoption by the
West so remarkable.

Mechanism	Impact on Latin Theology
Medieval Translations	His *Fountain of Knowledge* was translated into Latin by the 12th century, becoming a scholastic staple.
Scholastic Citations	Thomas Aquinas and other Latin theologians cited him as *Johannes Damascenus*, integrating his Christology and Trinitarian logic.
Council Reception	The **Second Council of Nicaea (787)**, which affirmed icon veneration, canonized his views—later accepted by the Latin Church.
Doctrinal Synthesis	His Aristotelian method and patristic harmonization offered a **template for systematic theology**, influencing Latin scholastics.

7. Thomas of Aquino: (1225-1274) Noble Blood, Noble Burden

Being of noble birth, the son of Landulph, Count of Aquino, and Theodora, Countess of Teano, Thomas entered the world not merely with pedigree, but with proximity to power. His lineage traced through Emperors Henry VI and II, and the royal houses of Aragon, Castile, and France. Yet it was not his ancestry that crowned him, it was his corpus: some 220 works, a literary cathedral whose stones were syllogism, sacrament, and scholastic framework.

He had few peers, if any, in his time. But even fewer interpreters who grasp the fault lines beneath his theological architecture.

Lexical Ledger of a Sacramental Architect

Thomas's vocabulary is not incidental—it is theological instrumentation. Consider the frequency and distribution of six key terms:

Term	Count	Locations	Notes
Testamentum	443	206	Often aligned with divine initiative and internal inspiration
Foedus	114	94	Thematically linked to opposition, demons, and infernal resistance
Pactum	169	108	Contractual nuance, occasionally sanctified

Term	Count	Locations	Notes
Feriam	26	25	Liturgical rhythm, feast and rest
Consummabo	10	7	Eschatological finality, tethered to Jeremiah 31 and Hebrews 8
Mediator	192	119	Christological bridge, but never covenantal ratifier in isolation

Throughout his works, these nouns and their verbal counterparts are often used interchangeably *testamentum, foedus, pactum* as if the semantic distinctions were subordinate to sacramental function. But this is precisely the problem.

Thematic Drift and Doctrinal Displacement

In *Scriptum super Sententiis*, Thomas employs *foedus* not to describe divine fidelity, but infernal opposition, demons, the devil, and negative influences. The covenant becomes a battlefield, not a bond. And while he addresses *Jeremiah 31* and *Hebrews 8*, he does so through the lens of sacramental visibility, not covenantal continuity.

He writes:

> *Praeterea, testamentum novum pertinere videtur ad internam inspirationem, ut patet ex hoc quod apostolus, ad Heb. VIII, introducit verba quae habentur in Ierem. XXXI: consummabo super domum Israel testamentum novum, dando leges in mentibus eorum. Sacramentum autem visibiliter agitur.*[57]

This is not covenant, it is **Catholic sacramentology**. The *testamen-tum novum* is not the product of divine oath, but the **external man-ifestation** of internal grace. The mediator is not the covenantal functionary, but the sacramental officiant.

The Missing Link

Thomas never reaches the conclusion that *mediator* is solely the functionary of covenant ratification. He sees the Scripture. He quotes it. He paraphrases it. But he cannot place it. The architecture of his theology cannot accommodate the scaffolding of Jeremiah's promise or Hebrews' fulfillment.

I offer as proof the following statement, one that reveals not igno-rance, but incompatibility. A system built for sacrament cannot house a covenant. And so the mediator remains suspended, neither priest nor guarantor, neither ratifier nor redeemer.

When God Became Greek: On the Displacement of Covenant by Testament

There is a distinct and irreducible difference between the ratifica-tion כָּרַתִּי of a covenant and the proposition *unitatem pacis facere* as the-ological intent. The former is a divine incision, a blood-bound oath cut into history. The latter is a philosophical aspiration, a gesture to-ward unity that lacks the blade.

It may be allowable, even tolerable, to treat *unitatem pacis* as con-tent for a *testamentum*, especially given Thomas's lexical habits. He as-sociates *foedus* and *pactum* with terms that imply written agreement *quam facit, compagin, quod pepigit, percussi*. But none of these are cog-nates of the Hebrew כָּרַתִּי. None carry the weight of severed flesh or sacrificial finality. They are not ratifiers, they are rhetorical scaffold-ing.

Thomas introduces these terms not as linguistic precision but as explanatory justifications for his theological position. He draws a con-nection between the *novum testamentum* and *Jeremiam*, stating there is a *brevis differentia*[58] a "slight difference" and that this difference is *sed ut praeparativum novae legis*. A preparatory sketch. A theological warm-up.

But this *praeparativum* is not benign. It forms a discontinuity, a rupture between the covenantal logic of Jeremiah and the sacramental architecture of Thomas. It is the product of a context he found himself in: one isolated from the Second Temple period, severed from the soil of Israel, and transplanted into the marble halls of Alexandria.

As Augustine before him, Thomas chose Alexandria, not Sinai, as his interpretive home. The **Hellenization of the covenants** was, by his time, complete. The Hebrew בְּרִית had been replaced by Latin *compagin*. The oath had become a document. The mediator had become a metaphysical bridge.

And yet no one asked: When did God become Greek? When did the Messiah take up residence on Mount Olympus? When did covenantal blood become philosophical ink?

These questions were not asked because the answers were inconvenient. They would have required a return, not to Rome, not to Alexandria, but to the cut pieces of Genesis 15, to the prophetic fire of Jeremiah 31, to the eschatological rupture of Hebrews 8.

But Thomas, for all his brilliance, never reached the conclusion that *mediator* is solely the functionary of covenant ratification. He saw the Scripture. He quoted it. He paraphrased it. But he could not place it. His system could not hold it.

And so the covenant remained, cut, but untranslated.

8. **John Wycliffe** (1320-1384)

On Wycliffe's Semantics: Smyte, Boond, and the Puple People

He used the cognomen *Jhesus* and *Jhesu Crist* for *Iesu Christi*. Not a mere orthographic whim, but a deliberate invocation of reverence in the vernacular tongue. This was Middle English, not yet fossilized, still pliable in the hands of a man who dared to smyte Latin's monopoly on sacred meaning. Foremost among these efforts was John Wycliffe, late fourteenth century, whose 1395 Bible will serve as our primary witness.

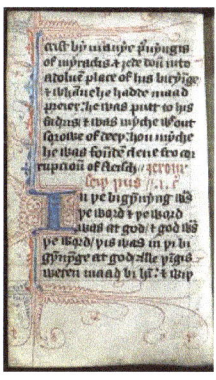

Wycliffe's semantic choices are best left to his own motives, as he expressed them with unapologetic clarity:

> "Christ and His Apostles taught the people in the language best known to them. It is certain that the truth of the Christian faith becomes more evident the more faith itself is known. Therefore, the doctrine should not only be in Latin but in the vulgar tongue... The laity ought to understand the faith... believers should have the Scriptures in a language which they fully understand."[59]

This is not a footnote. It is a theological earthquake. The man was not merely translating, he was transposing authority from clerical Latin to the entrails of the common soul.

Transmission of Tradition: LXX, Vulgata, and the Vernacular

The Wycliffe Bible of 1395 did not invent doctrine, it transmitted it. Faithfully, even provocatively, it carried the traditions of the Septuagint and the Vulgate into the Middle English vernacular. This is seen most vividly in a twofold examination of Jeremiah 31:31 and its fulfillment in Hebrews 8:8.

Jeremiah 31:31 (Wycliffe)

"Lo! daies comen, seith the Lord, and Y schal smyte a newe boond of pees to the hous of Israel, and to the hous of Juda."

Note the words: *smyte* and *boond*. He renders *covenant* as *boond*—a binding, yes, but also a bond. And *smyte*—not merely to cut, but to strike, to initiate with force. A covenant not whispered but hammered into history.

Hebrews 8:8 (Wycliffe)

For he repreuynge hem seith, Lo! daies comen, seith the Lord, and Y schal make perfit a **newe testament** on the hous of Israel, and on the hous of Juda;

Here the semantic shift begins. *Boond* becomes *testament*. *Smyte* becomes *make perfit*. The prophecy and its fulfillment diverge, not in spirit, but in diction. And diction, in theology, is never neutral.

The Semantic Rift: Jeremiah 31:34 vs. Hebrews 8:10

Let us press further into the semantic fault line.

Jeremiah 31:34 (Wycliffe)

And a man schal no more teche his neiybore, and a man his brother, and seie, Knowe thou the Lord; for alle schulen knowe me, fro the leeste of hem 'til to the mooste, seith the Lord; for Y schal be merciful to the wickidnessis of hem, and Y schal no more be myndeful on the synne of hem.

Hebrews 8:10 (Wycliffe)

But this is the testament, which Y schal dispose to the hous of Israel aftir tho daies, seith the Lord, in yyuynge my lawis in to the soulis of hem, and in to the hertis of hem I schal aboue write hem; and Y schal be to hem in to a God, and they schulen be to me in to a puple.

Now we must ask: Why *smyte* in Jeremiah, but *dispose* in Hebrews? Why *couenaunte* in prophecy, but *testament* in fulfillment? Why *entrails* in one, *soulis* in the other? And what, pray tell, is this *puple* people?

These are not mere translational quirks. One has to wonder why he chose smyte instead of a form of snithan? a reconstructed Middle English verb meaning "to cut" or "to strike with precision", and render its full conjugation across tense, mood, and person, using forms consistent with late 14th-century Wycliffite Middle English.

Unified Conjugation Table for *Snithan* (Middle English)

Mood/Tense	Person	Singular	Plural
Infinitive	—	*snithen*	—
Participle	—	*snithinge* (pres.) / *snet, isnet* (past)	—
Indicative	Present 1st	I *snithe*	We *snithen*
	Present 2nd	Thou *snitest*	Ye *snithen*
	Present 3rd	He/She/It *snithes*	They *snithen*
	Preterite 1st	I *snet*	We *snitten*
	Preterite 2nd	Thou *snettest*	Ye *snitten*
	Preterite 3rd	He/She/It *snet*	They *snitten*

Mood/Tense	Person	Singular	Plural
Subjunctive	Present	*snithe*	*snithen*
	Preterite	*snette*	*snitten*
Imperative	2nd Person	*snith*	*snitheth*
Compound Forms	—	*have snet* (perfect) / *is isnet* (passive)	—

They are theological decisions. Wycliffe is not just rendering text, he is rendering meaning. He is shaping the contours of covenantal continuity in a language that dares to breathe.

The Manuscript Debate: Hebrew, Greek, or Just Vulgate?

There are those who deny Wycliffe had access to Hebrew or Greek manuscripts. F.F. Bruce among them. They argue he worked solely from the Latin Vulgate. But Chapter 22 of *In Awe of Thy Word*, titled "Wycliffe's Views," claims otherwise:

> "John Wycliffe had the Hebrew Old Testament manuscripts which, along with the Greek exemplar, he used to 'correct the Vulgate', which brought his 'translations' into complete agreement with the Hebrew and Greek manuscripts."[60]

If true, this would make Wycliffe not merely a translator, but a textual reformer, correcting Rome with the raw materials of Jerusalem and Athens.

Conclusion: The Boond That Binds

Wycliffe's semantics are not accidents. They are provocations. *Smyte, boond, dispose, testament, puple* each word is a theological scalpel. He did not merely translate Scripture; he transfigured its accessibility.

And in doing so, he laid bare the covenant—not as a Latin relic, but as a living bond, smitten into the entrails of the people.

Let the laity read. Let the puple people rise.

Having concluded our select survey of the authors of the Middle Ages, those ecclesiastical scribes, monastic polemicists, and theological compilers whose ink often ran thicker than their exegesis, we now turn to the manuscripts themselves.

These texts, etched in the disciplined elegance of Carolingian Minuscule and preserved in the Anglo-Saxon tradition, are not mere relics of paleographic interest. They are ideological artifacts, each stroke a theological decision, each abbreviation a doctrinal gamble.

In both the authors previously cited and the manuscripts now under scrutiny, we present a comparative chart detailing how the phrase *"the cutting of a covenant"* or *"the cutting of the covenant"* was rendered, or misrendered, in Latin. This is not a stylistic indulgence but a necessary act of textual accountability. For in the translation of כָּרַת בְּרִית, the stakes are not grammatical—they are covenantal.

Too often I commiserate with Galadriel when she said, "And some things that should not have been forgotten were lost. History became legend. Legend became myth. And for two and a half thousand years, the Ring passed out of all knowledge."[61], [And so it is with the sacred, cut loose from its covenantal root, it drifts through the centuries like a relic misnamed. What was once a living bond becomes a footnote, then folklore, then fantasy. And we, heirs of the graft, are left sifting myth for memory, trying to remember what was never meant to be forgotten.

What may be illustrative of the slow sedimentation of interpretive consensus around Biblical motifs is not a sermon, nor a gloss, but a poetic contrast, one that Sir Gawain and the Green Knight (c. 1385–1390) provides with unsettling clarity. The poem does not merely echo covenantal themes; it refracts them through chivalric liturgy, rendering the hunt, the girdle, and the blade as sacramental signs.

How poetic it would have been—how fittingly tragic, had Joseph of Arimathea, that reluctant midwife of burial, foreseen the Vulgate Cycle not as a literary inevitability but as a prophetic burden. He, who bore the body of the Word, might have sought a nobler company than the ecclesial custodians of Latin hegemony. He might have fled to legend, not for escape, but for preservation—for legend offers a true timelessness, a genre unbound by papal imprimatur, where the once and future covenant may speak in meter and mystery.

Joseph, in this imagined exile, may have preferred the bob-and-wheel to the gloss and canon. For in the bob, one may confess. In the wheel, one may covenant. Against the external perceptions of these faraway lands, lands where covenant is reduced to contract and sacrifice to transaction, Joseph might have chosen the poetic as the last refuge of the sacred.

> "Now, sir Gawayn," sayde þe gome, "þis game is at an ende. I gef þe al þat I myght, and þou hatz wel þynges. I quyte þe quyte-clene... Þou art polyced and purged as clene as þou were born."[62]

This is no mere absolution, it is a liturgical pronouncement. The girdle, gold-hemmed and green, becomes a vestment of covenant. Gawain, confessed and purged, receives not just forgiveness but a renewal of identity. The edge of the blade is not punitive but purgative. The covenant is not annulled, it is fulfilled.

And while one might quibble at the application of covenant theology to what appears to be a simple image of the hunt, such quibbling betrays a failure to read sacramentally. The preparation of the carcass is not culinary, it is covenantal. As the men *"hewe hit in two,"* the reader is reminded of Abraham's divided animals, of the suzerain ritual that binds through blood. Bercilak's gift to Gawain is not hospitality, it is sacrifice. And the bargain they have made is not a game, it is a covenant.

In the opening tableau at Camelot, Gawain does not merely accept a challenge, he enters into covenant. Not a wager, not a dare, but a binding agreement sealed with time and blood: "a year and a day," the ancient metric of reckoning, after which he must receive the stroke of an axe. This is no idle flourish of chivalric sport. It is a type. A shadow. A prefiguration of the Last Judgement. The axe, suspended in narrative tension, becomes eschatological: Will it fall? Will it sever flesh from soul? Will Gawain's interim conduct—his sins, his concealments, his confessions—determine the outcome?

The Green Chapel scene is not merely climactic; it is liturgical. A particular sin is named. A penance is enacted. Forgiveness is granted. And in this, the poem offers more than allegory, it offers a model. A covenantal template for the Christian life, in which the believer lives not in abstraction but in anticipation. The possibility that one might "clene worþe" become clean, be made whole, is not a poetic flourish but a soteriological engine. The poem does not merely entertain; it instructs. It catechizes. Through reading, one might learn how to live in such a way that the axe, when it falls, does not condemn but confirms.

That this connection lay dormant, hidden in the folds of marginalia, obscured by the quest for narrative rather than covenant, should not surprise us. The academic guild, for all its footnotes and peer review, often misses the forest for the gloss. Yet even it, in its noble pursuits, occasionally stumbles upon truth. And when it does, it is not by accident, but by grace.

Ligatured Kings and Tonsured Scripts

The Merovingian ligatures were tangled, compressed, and aristocratically illegible, much like their final monarchs. Their script, like their rule, was ornate but increasingly inaccessible, a scribal aristocracy of curls and flourishes. Then came the Carolingians, wielding reform like a scalpel.

Enter Carolingian minuscule: clean, spacious, legible. It was not just a typographic innovation, it was a visual coup. Just as Pepin the Short tonsured Childeric III, stripping him of royal hair and sending him to a monastery, so too did the Carolingian scribes tonsure the page, shaving off the ligatures, compressions, and chaotic curls of Merovingian script.

- **Childeric III**: tonsured, cloistered, erased from power.
- **Merovingian ligatures**: snipped, simplified, erased from script.

The Carolingian minuscule didn't just replace a style, it redefined authority. The Carolingians didn't just tonsure Childeric III, they tonsured the page itself, shaving off the tangled ligatures of Merovingian script and replacing them with the clean, monastic clarity of Carolingian minuscule. And here's the twist of divine comedy: one of the most famous Merovingian ligatures comes from none other than Pope Gregory the Great's *Moralia in Job*, a text that would later be copied, canonized, and clarified in Carolingian script

To the north the Lindisfarne Gospels, born of insular mysticism and continental structure, would later be studied, copied, and even reinterpreted by Carolingian scribes, who sought clarity, order, and imperial theology. It's as if the manuscript itself was grafted into the Carolingian vine, much like Israel into the Gentiles.

Aldred's Old English gloss (added in the 10th century) often renders *testamentum* as *gesetnes* or *cyninges bebod*, emphasizing divine law and royal decree, subtly linking covenant to kingship and divine order. The carpet pages and cross motifs visually encode covenant as binding, woven, and sacrificial, a theology of blood and promise, not bureaucracy. The irony? The *same word* testamentum is visually and theologically refracted through two lenses: one mystical and tribal, the other imperial and systematic. And yet both traditions, in their own way, preserve the binding nature of divine promise.

So too was it that O! while William the Conqueror, through his maternal thread, bore the imperial tincture of Carolingian blood, a legacy baptized in the shadow of Charlemagne who himself had swallowed the Merovingian twilight like a sanctified leviathan, William came unto England not merely as a Norman duke but as a spectral heir to a twice-subsumed throne: Merovingian, then Carolingian, now Anglo-Saxon, each folded into the next like vellum beneath conquest. His sword bore the echo of imperial benediction, yet his boots muddied the soil of a kingdom whose saints had not asked for such a pedigree.

In all this the question remains.

What we should see:

English	Latin	Notes
1. He cut a covenant	Foedus secavit.	Perfect tense; general covenant
2. He will cut a covenant	Foedus secabit.	Future tense; general covenant
3. He cut the covenant	Foedus illum secavit.	Perfect tense; definite covenant (*illum* = "that" or "the")
4. He will cut the covenant	Foedus illud secabit.	Future tense; definite covenant (*illud* = "that" or "the")
5. He has cut the covenant	Foedus illud secavit.	Latin perfect = English perfect; same as #3
6. He has cut a covenant	Foedus quoddam secavit.	*quoddam* = "a certain" or "some" covenant; adds nuance

What did we see in this period:

Latin Phrase	Author / Source	Citation / Context
Foedus secavit	*Rarely attested directly*	No confirmed medieval author uses this exact phrase in surviving texts.
Foedus secabit	*No direct attestation found*	Future tense with *foedus* and *secare* is not standard in medieval Latin usage.
Foedus illum - secavit	*Seneca (not medieval)*	*De Brevitate Vitae* X.20.2: "Foedus ille..." used metaphorically

No exact matches are found in all the Latin corpus at the Perseus Digital Library.

Latin Phrase	Author / Source	Citation / Context
Foedus illud secabit	*No citation found*	No medieval manuscript or author currently known to use this construction.
Foedus illud sevavit	*Likely a typo for secavit*	No attestation found; if intended as *secavit*, see above.

Godescale Gospels

Carolingian Minuscule, ah, the imperial haircut of the page. Some 6,700-plus manuscripts survive, each one a quiet monument to the Carolingian obsession with clarity, order, and theological legibility. Among the most luminous is the Godescalc Gospels, a manuscript not merely copied but consecrated in ink, commissioned by Charlemagne himself on October 7th, 781, as if to say: *Let the Word be written in a hand worthy of empire.*

Preserved now in the Bibliothèque nationale de France, catalogued as NA. lat. 1203, it stands as a gilded witness to the moment when script became sacrament. Gold and silver ink on purple-stained vellum, this was not a book, it was a visual liturgy, a political theology in strokes and margins. Godescalc, the scribe-priest, did not merely write, he tonsured the page, just as Charlemagne had tonsured the Merovingian legacy, shaving off its tangled ligatures and cloistering its royal pretensions.

So the Godescalc Gospels are not just famous—they are symbolic, a typographic coronation, a covenantal scroll dressed in imperial vestments. And every minuscule letter whispers: *Rome is reborn, and the Word is now legible.* This was not a translation of the Gospels it was a selective liturgical device, meant to facilitate the Mass. The sad point is that looking to understand the notion of covenant is not possible with these manuscripts. This was not their intent. Their testimony was to the liturgy. This version furthered the Vulgata style, but not in script. This was a very important liturical adaptation of its day.

The next two manuscripts in the Anglo-Saxon tradition. First among them is the Anglo-Saxon Gospel Manuscript,[63] attributed to Ælfric around the year 1000, the word in question not *foedus*, not *testa-*

mentum, but cyþnes emerges with startling clarity, a native cognomen for divine bond.

- In Mark 14:24, the Eucharistic moment is refracted through Old English: *"Þis is mín blōd þæs nīwan cyþnesse, þe is for manegum āgyten."* Here, *cyþnesse* is not mere legal contract, it is witness, declaration, and sacrificial bond, poured out for many.
- In Luke 22:20, the covenantal cup is named again: *"Þes cuppe is sēo nīwe cyþnes in mīnum blōde, sēo þe bið for ēow āgyten."* The phrase echoes the Hebrew *berit* more than the Latin *testamentum*, it is relational, communal, and costly.
- And in Luke 1:72, the covenant is remembered as mercy: *"Þæt hē miltsian wolde ūrum fæderum, and gemunan his halgan cyþnesse."* Not a transaction, but a holy remembrance, a continuity of promise from Abraham to the grafted Gentile, or theologically Israelite.

The Second: The West Saxon Manuscript (c. 1175)[64] A Gospel book born of Alfredian legacy, not merely translated but transfigured, where covenantal language is rendered in the native tongue as *cyþnes*, a term that carries witness, blood, and memory in its marrow.

- Mark 14:24 Ða saide he heom þis is min blod þare nywe cyðnissan. þt beoð for manigen agoten.
- Luke 22:20 Ænd swa eac þanne calic; syððen he ge-eten hafde & cwæð. Þes calic is niwe cyðnis on minen blode se beoð for eow agoten.
- Luke 1:72 Mildheortnysse to werchen mid ure fæderen. & ge-munen hys halgan kyðnesse.

Form	Old English	Gloss	Function
Infinitive	cyðnissan	to cause to testify	Verbal root
Gerund	to cyðnissenne	in order to declare	Purpose clause
Present Participle	cyðnissende	declaring, testifying	Ongoing action
Past Participle	cyðnissod	testified, declared	Completed action
Imperative (2nd Sg)	cyðnissa	Declare!	Command
Imperative (2nd Pl)	cyðnissiaþ	Declare (you all)!	Plural command
Pres. Indic. 1st Sg	cyðnissie	I testify	Present action
Pres. Indic. 2nd Sg	cyðnissest	You declare	Present action
Pres. Indic. 3rd Sg	cyðniss(e)þ	He/she testifies	Present action
Pres. Indic. Pl	cyðnissiaþ	We/you/they declare	Present action
Pret. Indic. Sg	cyðnissode	I/you/he testified	Past action
Pret. Indic. Pl	cyðnissodon	We/you/they testified	Past action
Pres. Subj. Sg	cyðnissie	(that) I may testify	Hypothetical
Pres. Subj. Pl	cyðnissien	(that) they may declare	Hypothetical

Form	Old English	Gloss	Function
Pret. Subj. Sg	cyðnissode	(if) I had testified	Hypothetical
Pret. Subj. Pl	cyðnissoden	(if) they had declared	Hypothetical

Of particular interest, off topic, is the latter clause of Matthew 1:1 in Old English: *"Her is on cneornysse boc. hælendes cristes dauiðes suna. abrahames suna."* or in variant form *"Her is on cneornysse boc. hælendes cristes dauiðes suna. abrahame suna."*

The phrase **hælendes cristes** demands our attention—not merely for its poetic cadence, but for its theological audacity. This is no transliteration of the Latin *Jesu Christi* as found in the Vulgata. It is a deliberate departure, as in the Codex Amiatinus, a semantic incision. *Hælend* is not a name; it is a function. A title. A mission. It renders the Hebrew *Yeshua* not as a static proper noun, but as a dynamic covenantal role: "Savior," "Healer," "Deliverer." This is a topic not addressed by any scholarship, at least that I'm aware.

The Armenian Covenant as Vow and Consecration

Here, it would be of immense benefit to include the Armenian tradition, precisely because of its relative isolation from the theological and typographic conventions of Central and Western Europe. This isolation is not a deficit, it's a distinction. It allows the Armenian witness to offer a contrastive lens, a liturgical counterpoint, especially in its rendering of the Hebrew בְּרִית (*berit*) and its ratifier term for "cut."

The problem, however, is not merely semantic, it is typographic and infrastructural. The fonts and Unicode blocks required to faithfully render Armenian covenantal terms are incompatible with the Book Building Tool on IngramSpark's platform. The tool flattens the sacred into the generic. It cannot accommodate the glyph fidelity, the ligature integrity, or the semantic weight embedded in Armenian letter forms. What should be a theological act of publishing becomes a technical bottleneck.

And yet, even through these limitations, a deeper truth surfaces: the Armenian word most often chosen to render *berit* (*ukht*) is not a translation. It is a transfiguration. It morphs the juridical into the devotional. *Ukht* is not merely a covenant, it is a vow, a pilgrimage, a consecration. It absorbs the sacrificial and stretches it into the liturgical. It sanctifies the contract into a trajectory of devotion.

To include the Armenian tradition here is not just to compare, it is to expand. It is to allow the covenant to breathe in a different register, one shaped by vow, by offering, by incarnational fidelity.

Six

Re-inventing the wheel?

I'll be fine as soon as I wake up -- Alice[65]

During the Reformation, the question of who constituted the *covenanted people of God* fractured into competing visions. It was no longer a matter of ecclesial continuity, it became an inter-varsity struggle, a theological contest between Rome and the Reformers, each vying to define covenantal legitimacy. Martin Luther (1483–1546) and John Calvin (1509–1564) stood on opposite ends of this spectrum, not merely in tone but in theological architecture. This is another in a long line of reform movements. Another, let's return to our roots movements, just not Hebrew roots, that would be as Eric Idle exclaimed 'Are they too Jewish?' [66]

Luther's 1543 tract *On the Jews and Their Lies* reveals a tragic constriction of covenantal imagination. His rhetoric collapses the people of God into a polemic against Jewish identity, severing the Old Testament from its living heirs. The covenant becomes weaponized, its continuity denied, its bearers vilified. The ecclesial body is no longer grafted; it is amputated.

Calvin, by contrast, resists such reduction. He cannot be so easily placed in a theological category. His vision of covenant is broader, scriptural layered, and eschatologically charged. He reads the Testaments not as binaries but as a single unfolding drama of divine fidelity.

In his 1536 *Institutes of the Christian Religion*, Calvin writes:

> "Since God was pleased (and not in vain) to testify in ancient times by means of expiations and sacrifices that he was a Father, and to set apart for himself a chosen people, he was doubtless known even then in the same character in which he is now fully revealed to us."[67]

Here, Calvin refuses to bifurcate the Testaments. He sees בְּרִית (*berit*) not as abolished, but fulfilled, transposed into a new covenantal continuity. The people of God are not replaced; they are reconstituted, grafted, and sustained by the same divine breath that animated Abraham's oath and Christ's blood. This is not supersession, it is semantic grafting, a topological restoration of covenantal identity. This exposes the semantic gymnastics, where "fulfilled" is just a euphemism for "fired with theological flair." Quite like the theological version of ghosting, with divine justification.

It would seem that the Reformers, like those before them, couldn't resist the shears. They too reached for the pruning hook, eager to sever the 'natural branches' of the olive tree: the Jews. And all, allegedly, for the betterment of the faith. How sick is this? To mutilate the very tree that bore the covenantal root, and then call it flourishing.

But let's press the irony further. Can you even call it an olive tree if the natural branches are removed? Or is it now a theological topiary, shaped to suit the aesthetics of replacement?

And what of this modern impulse to 'graft in' the Jews under the rubric of evangelism? What are we grafting them into, exactly? A tree that has already disowned its native limbs? That's not restoration, it's theological taxidermy. The branch is not being welcomed home; it's being rebranded.

The olive tree of Romans 11 is not a metaphor for ecclesial conquest. It is a living witness to covenantal continuity. To treat the Jews as either obsolete or as targets for assimilation is to betray the very root that nourishes the Gentile grafts.

If the covenant is real, then the branches are not optional.

Returning to Calvin's statement, we are met with what can only be called a vain gesture in the presence of a revised testament. He writes:

> "Inasmuch as the term Gospel is applied by Paul to the doctrine of faith (II Timothy 4:10), it includes all the promises by which God reconciles men to himself, and which occur through the Law."[68]

But this is precisely the problem. Calvin affirms the Law as a vessel of promise, only to hollow it out in the next breath. He warns:

> "Here we must guard against the diabolical imagination of Servetus, who, from a wish, or at least the pretence of a wish, to extol the greatness of Christ, abolishes the promises entirely, as if they had come to an end at the same time with the Law."[69]

And yet, Calvin himself walks a tightrope between preservation and erasure. He is a proponent of theology within a dual interpretive category—not a protagonist like Luther, whose polemic against the Jews was unrelenting. Calvin is more surgical. He distinguishes between the Law's nature and its adventitious promises, claiming:

> "The Law everywhere contains promises of mercy; but as these are adventitious to it, they do not enter into the account of the Law as considered only in its own nature."[70]

This is a theological sleight of hand. The Law is reduced to a moral framework, commanding, prohibiting, rewarding, threatening, while its covenantal breath is treated as an accessory. Calvin attributes this view to Paul, constructing a framework of contrast between the Testaments, not continuity.

But here's the rupture: Calvin implies that the intent of the Old Testament was so that Yeshua could deliver the people from the Word of God. Not to fulfill it. Not to embody it. But to liberate them from it. This is not Romans 10, it is a theological inversion of it.

For Romans 10:8 declares:

"The word is near you, in your mouth and in your heart."

And why is it near? Because Paul is quoting Moshe. Not an abstraction. Not an "it."

"But what does it say?"

The "it" is Deuteronomy 30:11–14. The word of faith Paul preaches is not a rupture, it is a quotation. A retrieval. A grafting. It is a Word of Faith!

So what on earth is Paul doing by quoting the Old Testament? He is refusing to sever the root. He is refusing to treat Moshe as obsolete. He is refusing to let the covenant be pruned into oblivion.

Here's a typographic side-by-side comparison of the covenantal passage from Deuteronomy 30:11–14 in Hebrew script and its Pauline echo in Romans 10:5–7, rendered in both Koine Greek and English. This layout is framed for modular annotation, semantic mapping, and visual theology overlays:

A. Deuteronomy 30:11–14 (Hebrew Script)
(Masoretic Text)

כי המצוה הזאת אשר אנכי מצוך היום לא נפלאת היא ממך ולא רחוקה היא
לא בשמים היא לאמר מי יעלה לנו השמימה ויקחה לנו וישמענו אתה ונעשנה ולא
מעבר לים היא לאמר מי יעבר לנו אל עבר הים ויקחה לנו וישמענו אתה ונעשנה
כי קרוב אליך הדבר מאד בפיך ובלבבך לעשתו

B. Romans 10:5–7 (Koine Greek Script)

(Textus Receptus)

Μωυσης γαρ γραφει την δικαιοσυνην την εκ του
νομου οτι ο ποιησας αυτα ανθρωπος ζησεται εν
αυτοις η δε εκ πιστεως δικαιοσυνη ουτως λεγει
μη ειπης εν τη καρδια σου τις αναβησεται εις
τον ουρανον τουτ εστιν Χριστον καταγαγειν η
τις καταβησεται εις την αβυσσον τουτ εστιν
Χριστον εκ νεκρων αναγαγειν

C. Romans 10:5–7 (English Script)

(English Standard Version)

"For Moses writes about the righteousness that is based on the
law, that the person who does the commandments shall live by
them. But the righteousness based on faith says, 'Do not say in your
heart, "Who will ascend into heaven?"' (that is, to bring Christ
down) or 'Who will descend into the abyss?' (that is, to bring Christ
up from the dead)."

I need to point out, emphatically, that this is not, as it might appear, a diatribe aimed solely at Christendom. Judaism is complicit.
Not incidentally, not passively, but actively and strategically. It, Judaism, for its own ends, has been altogether duplicit in the promotion
of this stream of thought. Theological distancing masked as fidelity.
Social distancing masked as preservation. They too maintain a posture
of detachment, a kind of sanctified aloofness, all under the guise of
covenantal stewardship. But the grin gives it away, much like the
Cheshire Cat, they hover, smirking, above the fray they helped orches-
trate.

Their responses are often reactionary to Christendom. Many a once-held position, kneeling, for instance, was abandoned the moment it was adopted by the Church. And Isaiah 53? Functionally discarded. Either it's treated as if it doesn't exist, or its linguistic sinews are stretched so far they snap—grammar and syntax left bleeding on the floor of interpretive convenience.

Now, back to Deuteronomy 30. Isn't it ironic, no, providential, that this passage, near the end of the Torah, corresponds so precisely with Romans 10:4? It's not accidental. It's architectural. It illustrates that this is truly the goal, the τέλος of the Law. As Romans 10:4 declares: *"For Christ is the end (τέλος) of the law for righteousness to everyone who believes."*

But to translate τέλος as merely "end," as the KJV does, is not just misleading, it's contradictory.

- **a.** Because Romans 10:5–7 builds directly upon it.
- **b.** Because it flatly contradicts Yeshua's own words in Matthew 5:17: *"Do not think..."*, and yet they do.
- **c.** Because it rejects the relevance of Moshe, whom Yeshua affirms in John 5:46: *"For had you believed Moshe, you would have believed me: for he wrote of me."*

Note the phrasing: *believed Moshe*, not *believed in Moshe*. That's not a semantic accident, it's a technical prerequisite. Believing Moshe is the gateway to believing Yeshua. Reject Moshe, and you've already rejected the foundation.

Who knows, had this admonition been taken seriously, perhaps the Thirty Years' War might not have happened. The squabbling over their own versions, their own testaments, their own inheritances. This was inevitable, really. They abandoned the Hebraic covenantal status in order to war over the semantics of a *testament*, a term that itself betrays the relational architecture of Torah.

Erasmus

Desiderius Erasus Roterodamus (1466-1536) had lofty goals in his effort to produce a translation. Erasmus, not the caricatured humanist of popular imagination, but the textual craftsman who dared to challenge the Vulgate's monopoly. His *Novum Instrumentum Omne*, first printed in Basel in 1516, was not merely a bilingual Greek-Latin New Testament. It was a typographic rupture. A theological scalpel.

He declared - 'It is only fair that Paul should address the Romans in somewhat better Latin.' [71]

His scholarly compass remained fixed on the apostolic terrain of the New Testament, culminating in the *Novum Instrumentum Omne*

Erasmus

(1516), a typographic watershed. There, Erasmus unveiled the first printed edition of the Greek New Testament, flanked by his own Latin revision, not as a mere parallel text but as a polemical counterpoint to the Vulgate's hegemony.

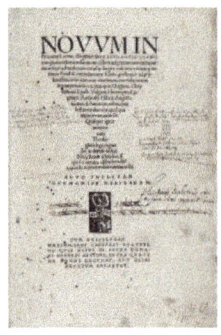

His Latin version of Hebrews 8:8,10

Hebrews 8:8

Vituperans enim eos dicit: Ecce dies veniunt, dicit Dominus, et consum-
mabo super domum Israel et super domum Iuda testamentum novum.

Hebrews 8:10

Hoc est enim testamentum quod disponam domui Israel post dies illos,
dicit Dominus: Dabo leges meas in mentem eorum, et in cordibus eorum
scribam eas: et ero eis in Deum, et ipsi erunt mihi in populum.

As this was one of the earliest printed editions of the Greek New
Testament, it bears noting that the printer was Johann Froben
(1460–1527), a man whose press in Basel became the crucible for Erasmus's textual restoration. The *Novum Instrumentum Omne* was not just
a scholarly triumph, it was a commercial one. It outsold all contenders
and was published prior to the Complutensian Polyglot, drawing what
was said to be "much ire from Spain." [72] That ire was not merely
nationalistic, it was theological. The Spanish scholars had labored for
years on their Polyglot, only to be preempted by Erasmus's leaner,
sharper edition.

This version became the consensus text in northern Europe, and by
the time the *Authorized Version* (AV), the King James Bible, was produced, Erasmus's edition was considered normative. It formed the textual backbone for the Luther Bible, the Tyndale Bible, and ultimately
the AV itself. It was not just a source, it was a standard.

Of these, the Tyndale version stands out with particular gravity.
William Tyndale (1492–1536) was a man of devotion and sincerity,
qualities that demand honor, not sentimentality. He, like Wycliffe before him, was a scholar of sound courage. But there is a subtle distinction worth noting: Wycliffe's conflict with the Church was primarily
doctrinal. Tyndale's conflict, however, was textual. His quarrel with
the Church and with Henry VIII was over the Scriptures themselves,
their accessibility, their language, their authority.

Tyndale believed the Word should be heard in the tongue of the ploughboy, not locked behind Latin. His translation was not just linguistic, it was covenantal. He was restoring what had been withheld. And for that, he paid with his life.

in 1535 from his prison cell Tyndale said

"Wherefore I beg of your lordship, and that by the Lord Jesus, that if I am to remain here through the winter you will request the commissary to have the kindness to send me from the goods of mine which he has a warmer cap, for I suffer greatly from the cold in the head and am afflicted by a perpetual catarrh, which is much increased in this cell. A warmer coat also, for this which I have is very thin. A piece of cloth, too, to patch my leggings. My overcoat is worn out. My shirts are also worn out. He has a woolen shirt, if he will be good enough to send it. I have with him also leggings of thicker cloth to put on above. He also has warmer night caps. And I ask to be allowed to have a lamp in the evening. It is indeed a wearisome to sit alone in the dark. But most of all I beg and beseech your clemency to be with the commissary that he will kindly permit me to have the Hebrew Bible, Hebrew grammar, and Hebrew dictionary, that I may pass the time in that study. In return may you obtain that which you most desire so only that it be for the salvation of your soul. But if any other decision has been taken concerning me to be carried out before winter, I will be patient. Abiding the will of God to the glory of the grace of my Lord Jesus Christ, whose Spirit I pray may ever direct your heart. Amen William Tyndale."[72]

Had he but received the above, his Hebrew Bible, Grammar, and Dictionary, and not the fate below, what would have been?

execution of Tyndale

On the morning of 6 October 1536, now in the hands of the secular forces, he was taken to the place of execution, tied to the stake, strangled and burned. His last words reportedly were: 'Oh Lord, open the King of England's eyes.'[73]

His toungue of Hebrews was:

[74]Hebrews 8:8 For in rebukynge the he sayth: Beholde the dayes will come (sayth the lorde) and I will fynnyshe apon the housse of Israhel and apon the housse of Iuda

8:10 *For this is the* testament *that I will* make *with the housse of Israhell: After those dayes sayth the lorde: I will put my lawes in their myndes and in their hertes I will wryte the and I wilbe their God and they shalbe my people.*

Is the above so rude as to question its toungue? His translation of Hebrews does not accord with Jeremiah, a text he never reached, never rendered. So where, precisely, was the foundation laid? Daniel writes:

> "In Europe, rabbinical schools flourished and knowledge of Hebrew was growing. Tyndale learned Hebrew: perhaps in Worms, the main centre of Jewish learning in Germany. Hebrew was almost unknown in England."[75]

Surely it was in the Altstadt, in the Judengasse of Worms, where he vanished into the woodwork. That was the season of scrutiny, when both he and the Jewish community lived under threat, restriction, and silence. Yet no rabbinic responsa, no communal ledger, no memoir from Worms names him. No trace. No witness.

And here the question sharpens: the rabbinic sources of SHuM, those pillars of Ashkenazic halakhah, would not have drawn a semantic line from *brit* (בְּרִית) to *testament*. That link is foreign to their covenantal lexicon. So why, in light of his theological rupture with Rome over *ekklesia*, choosing *congregation* over *church*, did he still retain *testament*?

Was it reverence? Was it oversight? Or was it the residue of a Latin frame he could not fully shed?

The mystery remains. And the silence of Worms speaks louder than its archives. Would he have known of the Johannes Reuchlin's *De Rudimentis Hebraicis* (1506)?

It should be noted, and with no small measure of precision, that today the Brown-Driver-Briggs, Strong's Concordance, and HALOT do not list *testament* as the or even a meaning of בְּרִית (*brit*). The term is consistently rendered as *covenant*, *pact*, or *alliance*, with lexical emphasis on relational binding, ritual enactment, and theological continuity. "Testament," as it appears in English theological discourse, is a translational artifact, not a semantic root. To conflate the two is to collapse the blood-bound mutuality of *brit* into the juridical finality of a last will, a move that obscures rather than reveals the covenantal architecture of Scripture. One has to wonder, truly, about the theological eyewear worn by certain scholars, the kind of interpretive lenses so tinted with tradition that they manage to see the Hebrew word בְּרִית (*brit*) as meaning "testament" even when staring directly at a lexicon that says otherwise.

What can we deduce from these Scripture portions? What was Tyndale's understanding of the institution of the *congregation*, not merely as a social assembly, but as a covenantal body? He just does not address the foundational structure referenced in Jeremiah 31, Hebrews 8, nor Ephesians 2:11–18. These are not peripheral texts, they are architectural. They define the covenantal reconstitution of Israel and the grafting in of the nations. And yet, in The Obedience of a Christian Man (1528), A Brief Declaration of the Sacraments (1533), The Practice of the Prelates (1530), and The Parable of the Wicked Mammon (1528), we find no direct engagement with these passages.

It is only within An Answer to Sir Thomas More's Dialogue that we glimpse an allusion. The first appears as follows:

"Whereon Paul saith (Eph. ii.) that we are built, and thereby of the household of God. And this is the rock, whereon Christ built his." [76]

The second:

"But they only that repent, and feel that the law is good, and have the law of God written in their hearts, and the faith of our Savior Jesus, even the Spirit of God." [77]

These statements raise a question: is Tyndale alluding to a characteristic of the church, or an analogy? There is no explicit ecclesiology here, no structural theology of the *ekklesia* as covenantal fulfillment. The notion that the Church of Rome was not central or critical for the contextual understanding of Scripture would have been, in his time, a foreign concept. And yet, Tyndale's translation has taken its place on the stage, shaping the vernacular, scaffolding the Reformation, and reconfiguring the theological imagination.

Let us summarize the textual landscape of his era:

Comparative Table of "Covenant" Terminology in Early Reformation Bibles

Bible Version	Year	Jeremiah 31:31	Jeremiah 31:33	Hebrews 8:8	Hebrews 8:10
Luther's NT (German)	1522			Testament	Testament
Tyndale's NT	1526			*fynnyshe* (shift to v.9)	testament (make)
Coverdale Bible	1535	*Couenaunt* (make)	*Couenaunt* (make)	*fynish* (shift to v.9)	Testament (make)

Bible Version	Year	Jeremiah 31:31	Jeremiah 31:33	Hebrews 8:8	Hebrews 8:10
Great Bible	1540	*Couenaunt* *(made)*	Counaunt *(make)*	fynyssh *(shift to v.9)*	testament *(make)*
Matthew's Bible	1537	*Couenaunt* *(make)*	*Couenaunte* *(make)*	fynyshe *(shift to v.9)*	testament *(make)*
Bishop's Bible	1568	*Couenaunt* *(make)*	*Couenaunt* *(make)*	*Couenaunt* *(finishe)*	couenaunt *(make)*
Geneva Bible	1599	*Couenaunt* *(make)*	*Couenant* *(make)*	*testament* *(make)*	Testament *(make)*

The last thousand years of translation have wandered far afield from the prophetic Hebrew intent—what was coming, not what was institutionalized. From the Vulgata to Tyndale, the cutting of a covenant -כָּרַת בְּרִית, has been a non-factor, eclipsed by the sacraments, embalmed in ecclesiology. The blade has been dulled. The blood, abstracted.

The translators, those stewards of sacred text, have failed to grasp the death clause of covenant. And this failure is not minor. It is inexcusable.

How can one speak of the death of a singular testator when Hebrews 9:17 uses the plural: επι νεκροις, "upon dead bodies"? Not νεκρός, singular. Not metaphor. But plural masculine dative- νεκροις. The covenant is ratified not by the death of one man, but by corpse plurality—a ritual echo of Genesis 15, where animals are severed and the divine presence passes through the pieces.

So how many bodies did the testator of the New Covenant have? Scott W. Hahn writes:

"If indeed the author was intending to speak of the death of the testator, the phrase is awkward, especially the use of the plural (νεκροις, 'dead [bodies]')."[78]

And he's right to call it awkward. But awkwardness is not error, it is resistance. The text resists the sacramental gloss. It demands covenantal reckoning.

The Abingdon Strong's Exhaustive Concordance, so-called, lists *G3498* but omits the ending *-οις*. It offers the lemma, but not the morphology. It gives the singular, but not the plural. It gives the abstraction, but not the ritual. This is not exegesis, it is evasion.

The translations do not present the context for why this question is vital. They do not ask: Why was it necessary for Yeshua to die? Not as martyr. Not as moral exemplar. But as ratifier, as the one who walks between the pieces.

This is the rabbit hole into which we have fallen. Not Alice's Wonderland, but a theological oubliette, where covenantal death is forgotten, and testamentary abstraction reigns.

Seven

The Word of the King

White Rabbit cried out 'Silence in the court!' and the King put on his spectacles and looked anxiously round, to make out who was talking' [79]

King James I

We have now come to the Millenary Petition of 1603. It should be no wonder that this would not happen. After a millennium and a half of faulty hermeneutics, layer upon layer of misreadings, mistranslations, and theological sleight-of-hand, it's a wonder this did not erupt sooner. The irony is thick: that a group calling themselves *Puritans*, a reformist sect nestled within the very ecclesial structure they sought to purify, would draft a petition to the King of England -

The Petition:

"Most gracious and dread sovereign, Seeing it has pleased the Divine majesty, to the great comfort of all good Christians, to advance your highness, according to your just title, to the peaceable government of this Church and Commonwealth of England, we, the ministers of the gospel in this land, neither as factious men affecting a

popular parity in the Church, nor as schismatics aiming at the disso-
lution of the State ecclesiastical, but as the faithful servants of Christ
and loyal subjects to your majesty, desiring and longing for the redress
of divers abuses of the Church, could do no less in our obedience to
God, service to your majesty, love to His Church, than acquaint your
princely majesty with our particular griefs;"[80]

From 1604 to 1611 we have the [not so] Authorized Version, what
would come to be known as the King James Version (KJV), in pro-
duction. Arguably the most well-known of the English translations today, though its fame is more cultural than covenantal. At its core, this
translation was born not from a hunger for restoration, but from a
royal response to a plea: the Puritans' demand for "redress of diverse
abuses of the Church."[81] A phrase that rings with ecclesial irony.

These so-called "abuses" four primary categories outlined in
the Millenary Petition, were not anomalies. They were mirrors. Re-
flections of a deeper structural malaise. The Puritans, earnest as they
were, mistook symptoms for sickness. They diagnosed liturgical excess, vestments, and ecclesiastical hierarchy as the disease, when in
truth these were the visible outgrowths of a compromised root system.

Their "concerns"[82] bracketed in piety, form a composite image of
the church itself as the problem, not merely its practices.

The Four Issues.
1) In the Church service:
2) Concerning Church ministers:
3) For Church livings and maintenance:
4) For Church discipline:

With this, the point they missed was not liturgical excess or clerical
misalignment, it was an institutional malady. A sickness in the bones
of the ecclesial body. To demand a Scripture that would correct defects is to indict the very conventions that birthed those defects. It

is to question not only the theology but the machinery, the administration, the social architecture, the ontological assumptions about authority itself.

To commission a translation under royal decree is to attribute an ontologically relational position to the monarch. The King becomes not merely patron but proxy, standing in the liminal space between divine utterance and vernacular reception. The historical record does not shy from this: the chronological neatness of biblical transmission, bracketed so precisely around Elizabeth's reign, is not coincidence. It is social agency masquerading as providence. I doubt the Puritans, bound by their feudal worldview, grasped this. It was a mute point to them. But it was no less true.

And so, one must take care what one asks for. Because you might just get it.

In response, James convened the Hampton Court Conference in 1604. A gathering not of prophets, but of policy-makers. The result: a decree to produce a vernacular translation. But was Hampton Court the hinge? The moment we moved from Reformation to post-Reformation perception? Did the primacy of polity be-

Hampton Court

gin to fracture under the weight of hermeneutical inquiry? Westminster, Cambridge, Oxford, did they challenge the crown, or reinforce it?

The presence of Hebraists like Wakefield, Lively, Buxtorf, and Drusius among the philologists of the day opened the door. But they did not walk through it. The driving force was not their scholarship, it was the rules. Six companies, one set of instructions. And among them, rule three stands out like a scar:

> "The old ecclesiastical words be kept" such as *church* instead of *congregation*.

This was not a neutral choice. It was partisan. It predetermined the outcome. It reinforced associations so deeply that exceptions became glaring. Context was quarantined from inquiry. Those who saw the problem had to wait. And wait.

For the First Oxford Company and the Second Westminster Company, this rule was untenable. Their apportioned texts made fidelity impossible. Rule three did not preserve tradition, it formalized an anachronism. Did the disciples of our Lord use "old ecclesiastical words"? Or did they speak in the language of covenant, not cathedral?

Those who sought the message were relegated to the margins. The political role of the KJV was not incidental, it was theatrical. As Hamlet said, "The play's the thing wherein I'll catch the conscience of the King."[83] And indeed, the translation became a stage. A performance of unity, masking fragmentation.

With the turmoil of James and Charles Stuart, and the rise of Cromwell, the associations embedded in the translation became a profound influence on scholarship. To understand the KJV, one must look not only at the text, but at the companies. Their composition, their assignments, their constraints. The translation was not merely a linguistic artifact. It was a theological mirror, framed by politics, polished by compromise.

Company Assignment Table

First Oxford Company		Second Westminster Company	
Isaiah to Malachi		Epistles	
John Harding		William Barlow	*
John Reynolds	^	John Spencer	

First Oxford Company	Second Westminster Company
Thomas Holland ^	Roger Fenton
Richard Kilby	Ralph Hutchinson
Miles Smith	William Dakins
Richard Brett	Michael Rabbet
Daniel Fairclough	Thomas Senderson
William Thorne	Nicholas Felton
Richard Fairclough	Arthur Lake
	Nicholas Love
	George Ryves
	John Overall
^ = Puritan * = anti Puritan	

How could rule number three "the old ecclesiastical words be kept" possibly apply to the prophetic context of Jeremiah, especially under the purview of the First Oxford Company? It's a category error of the highest order. Jeremiah is not a bishop's manual. It is covenantal lament, divine indictment, and eschatological hope. To impose ecclesiastical terminology onto the prophets of Israel is to graft foreign limbs onto a living tree. The result is not restoration, it's distortion.

Even if one were to interpret the Epistles through the lens of Second Temple Judea, the contextual dissonance between the First Oxford and Second Westminster Companies becomes glaring. There is no hermeneutical bridge that spans the chasm between prophetic Hebrew and post-Resurrection Greek ecclesiology. There simply could not be any "old ecclesiastical words" in the mouths of prophets who stood outside the temple gates, calling Israel back to covenant, not to polity.

To read ecclesiastical polity into the Tenach is to read one's own institutional reflection into the sacred text. It is not exegesis, it is projection. And herein lies the deeper malady: self-perception as hermeneutic. Authorized, no less, by James I under the banner of the "divine right of kings." The monarch becomes the lens, the arbiter, the theological anchor. But this is not fidelity, it is fiat.

The rules, drawn up by Archbishop Richard Bancroft, were not neutral. They were preemptive strikes against Puritan influence. Yet their consequences were more insidious: they became hermeneutical constraints. They shaped not just the translation, but the interpretive posture of the entire project. It's as if someone wrote a sequel to *Back to the Future* and cast Dr. Emmett Brown as a theologian. The absurdity is not amusing, it's tragic. Because this is not an answer. It's a performance.

In what sense can one alter the qualifying verb of its subject and not see that fulfillment is severed? Jeremiah's text is not a canvas for ecclesiastical brushstrokes. It is a cry from the covenantal deep. To tamper with its verbal architecture is to fracture its eschatological spine. And so, the text of Jeremiah becomes contested ground all over again, not because of its content, but because of the rules imposed upon its transmission.

It is time we looked closely—unflinchingly, at four verses, rendered exactly as the 1611 translators inscribed them in the blackletter script of their moment. Not modernized. Not softened. But preserved in the typographic breath of their ecclesiastical constraint. These verses are not merely textual artifacts; they are theological battlegrounds where covenantal fidelity collides with royal prerogative.

Let us begin:

Jeremiah 31:31 (1611) *Behold, the dayes come, saith the Lord, that I will* **make** *a new Couenant with the house of Israel, and with the house of Iudah:*

Jeremiah 31:33 (1611) *But this shall bee the Couenant that I will* **make** *with the house of Israel, After those dayes, saith the Lord, I will put my law in their inward parts, and write it in their hearts, and will bee their God, and they shall be my people.*

Hebrews 8:8 (1611) *For finding fault with them, he saith, Behold, the dayes come, saith the Lord, when I will* **make** *a new Couenant with the house of Israel, and with the house of Iudah:*

Hebrews 8:10 (1611) *For this is the Couenant that I will* **make** *with the house of Israel after those dayes, saith the Lord, I will put my lawes into their minde, and write them in their hearts, and I will bee to them a God, and they shall be to me a people:*

By 1611, the Authorized Version was complete. A translation in what was then modern English, though "modern" is always a moving target. This version, like every one before it, was as much a mirror of its culture as it was a window into Scripture. It bore the fingerprints of its time, its politics, its ecclesiology, and most tellingly, its linguistic assumptions.

The Anglicization of names in the KJV is a case study in transliteration gone rogue. The etymological integrity of biblical names was not merely compromised, it was evacuated. Names were stretched, bent, and rebranded until they bore more resemblance to English nobility than to Semitic origin. The result? A congregation reading aloud with confidence, yet unknowingly reciting a cultural parody. It's almost comical. One imagines "James," the half-brother of the Lord Yeshua, not in sandals but in a tartan kilt, perhaps playing bagpipes instead of the shofar. The irony is thick: the name *James* doesn't even appear in the biblical record until its late twelfth-century Scottish emergence. And yet, there he is, canonized by culture, not covenant.

The pronoun structure of the 1611 version is another relic of its feudal scaffolding. *Thee, thou, ye,* not merely linguistic flourishes, but social indicators. They encode hierarchy, deference, and relational distance. Useful in a courtly society, perhaps. But for modern readers, they are stumbling blocks, linguistic fossils that obscure rather than illuminate.

The King, of course, was declared head of the Church. But what does that mean functionally? Was he a theological mediator? A linguistic gatekeeper? A governing principle for translation itself? These are not idle questions. They strike at the heart of the dissatisfaction that plagued the first half of the sixteenth century. The proliferation of versions was not a sign of clarity, it was a symptom of unrest.

And then there are the marginal notes. Often overlooked, but never insignificant. They are the quiet confessions of the translators—moments where certainty falters and ambiguity creeps in. Consider:

1. **Hebrews 8:6** – *Covenant: or, Testament*
2. **Hebrews 8:10** – *put: Gr. give*
3. **Hebrews 8:10** – *in: or, upon*
4. **Jeremiah 31:32** – *although I was a husband unto them: or, should I have continued a husband unto them?*

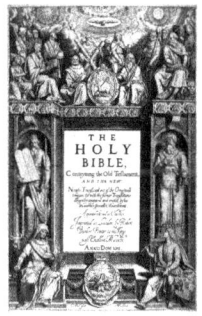

1611 Cover

These notes are not mere footnotes. They are theological fault lines. Each one reveals a tension between fidelity and tradition, between linguistic precision and ecclesiastical expectation. The note on Jeremiah 31:32 is especially telling—it questions the very nature of divine covenantal continuity. Was God a husband? Should He have remained one? The translators knew the stakes. And they left breadcrumbs.

John Reynolds, president of Corpus Christi College, Oxford, and a member of the First Oxford Company, urged a change in policy toward authorized biblical translations, arguing that *"those which were al-*

lowed in the raignes of Henry the eight, and Edward the sixt, were corrupt and not answerable to the Originall."[84] This is exasperating, almost maddening, when held against the clarity and conviction of William Tyndale, who decades earlier had already pierced the veil of ecclesiastical gatekeeping. Tyndale wrote: *"They will say it cannot be translated into our tounge it is so rude. It is not so rude as they are false lyers. For the Greeke tounge agreeth more with the English, then wyth the Latin. And the properties of the Hebrue tounge agreeth a thousand tymes more wyth the Englishe, then wyth the Latyn."[85]* Tyndale understood what Reynolds and his contemporaries were still debating: that fidelity to the original languages was not a technical problem, it was a theological imperative.

What occurred in the wake of these debates, whether by coincidence or providence, was a political stabilization that allowed for a new kind of intellectual emergence. A sense and sensibility I would call *extroception*: the turning outward of theological inquiry, the recognition that Scripture speaks not only to the soul but to the structure of society. The Hebraists were rising among the philologists. Hermeneutics was no longer a clerical tool, it was becoming a cultural force.

The works of John Lightfoot and John Weemse must be measured not only by their academic rigor but by their resonance within the homilies, hymnology, and literature of their time. Their influence was not confined to the university, it permeated the pulpit and the pew. Jai-Sung Shim's thesis[86] on Weemse is exhaustive, and rightly so. But the question remains: was biblical context given primacy over social convention? The answer, I believe, lies in their vocabulary. Words like *covenant* and *mediator* do not appear by accident, they are the fruit of theological labor, the residue of a hermeneutic that sought alignment with the divine narrative.

Shim's proposition that *"Protestant theologians of the sixteenth and seventeenth centuries understood Scripture as the living Word of God that is true and normative for the contemporary church"[87]* raises a deeper question: how is this justified by the claim that *"the true Orthodox Christian*

Church"[88] is the basis of biblical interpretation and prophecy? Just how many prophets of Israel were ordained as orthodox prelates? The question is not rhetorical, it is historical. The prophets were covenantal disruptors, not institutional custodians.

Was Weemse's approach different in kind or degree? That's the hinge. His first major work, *The Christian Synagogue[89]*, is emblematic of the modern Messianic movement's struggle. Like many today, Weemse sought to recover the Hebraic roots of Christian theology. But unlike many today, he understood that the Word of God functions as a whole, not as a buffet of doctrinal curiosities. The modern movement has not yet reached the level of integration Weemse achieved. The paradigm remains fragmented, caught in the condition of κνηθόμενοι (itching ears) and ηνακοην (novelty-seeking), as warned in Acts 17:21 and 1 Corinthians 2:4.

Too often, what is sought is entertainment, not transformation. A life not shaped by the message of the Kingdom, but distracted by theological ornamentation. Lightfoot, for all his brilliance, never directly quoted Jeremiah 31:31–34 or Hebrews 8. But the question remains: did he operate within the same hermeneutical and eschatological framework as the Apostle Shaul (Paul)? His use of the word *sacrament*, defined within a dispensational schema, lacks the continuity Paul expressed. It fractures the covenantal arc.

Would Shaul (Paul) have written as John Lightfoot states:

'VI. *The new testament in my blood.* So our evangelist and so the apostle, 1 Corinthians_11 with reference to the whole ministry of the altar, where blood was poured out; nay, with respect to the whole Jewish religion, for here was the beginning or entry of the new covenant. And indeed it seems that the design of that frequent communion of the Lord's supper in the first ages of the church, among other things, was, that those who were converted from Judaism might be sealed and confirmed against Judaism; the sacrament itself being the mark of the cessation of the old testament and the beginning of the new.' [90]

The invocation of "sacrament" by Paul would have been an anachronism, anachronistic not merely in terminology but in conceptual architecture. Paul did not operate within the ecclesial frameworks later codified by Westminster or Trent; his lexicon was covenantal, his praxis rabbinic, his theology apocalyptic. To retroject sacramental categories onto Pauline texts is to flatten the semantic terrain he inhabited.

John Weemse's division of his volumes under the rubric of *Divine Law* as subject matter, while ingenious in its Reformation-era scaffolding, was not Paul's doing. Nor was the Torah apportioned as a systematized work in the apostolic age. The rabbinical cataloging of the *Mitzvot*, those 613 commandments, was a post-Temple taxonomy, not reflected in the structure of the *Talmud* nor the *Mishnah*, which themselves are layered dialectics rather than linear codes.

The theological grammar of Westminster, Oxford, and Cambridge did not descend from heaven but was projected to the masses through homilies, hymns, and synods, liturgical echoes of scholastic scaffolding. One has but to survey the volumes of sermons by William Beveridge (1637–1708) of Cambridge. Beveridge did not merely preach; he transmitted the doctrinal architecture of his age in pulpit form. His sermons, contained in the first of five volumes within the twelve-volume set of *The Theological Works of William Beveridge, D.D.*[90]

Sermons:

Likely delivered during his tenure as **Bishop of St. Asaph**
(1704–1708)

Sermon **XXIX** entitled 'Christ the Savior to All That Come To Him'

the following citation in the margin of Jeremiah 31:33 he states 'When God hath written His law in their hearts, so as they themselves are inclined to it, it follows in course, that they go to Christ, and so become His people.'

Sermon **XXX** entitled 'Christ the Only Mediator' II Timothy 2:5

the quote: '... Christ's Mediation for us, it will be necessary to look back upon the first establishment of these two covenants, especially the latter, upon which it is founded.'

Sermon **XLVIII** entitled 'The Communion of Saints' Eph. 2:19

the quote: 'They have the one Mediator between God and men, always appearing in the presence of God, and making intercession for them, and for none but them'

Sermon **LXVIII** entitled 'The Mystery of our Reconciliation by Christ Explained' II Corinthians 5:18,19

quote: 'For He is our peace, who hath broken down the middle wall of partition between us, having abolished in His flesh the enmity'

Sermon **CIV** entitled 'The Nature, Extent, and Polity of God's Kingdom on Earth' part 3

That we Christians are as much bound to obey the commands he lays upon us now, as the Jews under the old covenant were. What difference there is, is wholly and solely on God's part; who, instead of expecting obedience from us, is pleased, in this new covenant, to give this obedience to us. Instead of saying, 'Do this and live,' he hath, in effect, said, I will enable you to do this, that so you may live. 'I will put my laws into your minds, and write them in your hearts; and I will be to you a God, and you shall he to me a people. - reference by him on Hebrews 8:10

Questions

In review of his sermons a few questions are necessary.

Did Beveridge make the point that the mediation was equated with Messiah being the sacrifical lamb or offering as the 'Old Testament' required?

How many members of the various companies that were commissioned to produce the Authorized version by James of the same position as Beveridge in this regard?

So how did he deal with the notion that a testator and a mediator had been conflated for so very long?

Did he rejected the position that Christ was a testator as a testament required?

Did Beveridge make the point that the mediation was equated with Messiah being the sacrifical lamb or offering as the Old Testament required?

In all his sermons did he state or imply that a covenant was the result of mediation and not the result of using the words made or make?

"The covenant is, not that he will be our God, *if* we will be his people, but he *will* be our God, and we *shall* be his people. But still, all this is *in and through Christ*, the surety and mediator of this covenant, in whom all the 'promises are yea and amen'... so that Christ may be looked upon, not only as a surety, but as a *party* in this covenant of grace..."[91]

It would appear that Beveridge, having a similar affinity with Lancelot Andrewes and John Overall, participated in a quiet but deliberate recentering of biblical context, one that gestured toward the Tenach not as antecedent, but as architectural. Their theological posture did not merely honor the Hebrew Scriptures; it enfolded the apostolic writings into its covenantal frame, treating the whole as one Book, not two testaments stitched together.

This was not a flattening of distinction, but a restoration of continuity. Andrewes, with his liturgical gravitas, and Overall, with his doctrinal precision, shared Beveridge's instinct: that the grammar of divine speech, promise, mediation, ratification, was already fully alive in the Tenach, and that the writings of the disciples were not a departure but a fulfillment within that same covenantal logic.

What emerges is not a rupture but a rethreading. The disciples do not overwrite the prophets; they echo them. The New does not replace the Old, it reveals its inner structure. Beveridge and his circle, in their sacramental fidelity and theological rigor, helped reorient the Church toward this unity. Not by decree, but by example. Not by polemic, but by liturgical and exegetical weight.

His sermons contained the Scriptural actuality, not mere theological abstraction, but the reinforcing statement of two aspects of *enmity*: being both abolished and slain. This duality, though exegetically evident, has had little presence in the last four centuries, where the flattening of covenantal categories has rendered such distinctions theologically inconvenient. Yet these sermons bore within them the marrow of covenant understanding, the very architecture upon which the preaching of the Kingdom of God must be built.

The question remains whether the seventeenth-century context permitted the comprehension of the incorporative nature of the *commonwealth of Israel*. For in that era, Israel was not treated as a covenantal polity but as an allegorical cipher, an ecclesial metaphor, stripped of legal substance. It had no juridical standing, no covenantal reality. The statement in Ephesians 2:11, "ye were at that time without Christ, being aliens from the commonwealth of Israel", is cast in the past tense, yet that condition remained experientially unaltered for both Judaism and Christendom. The ecclesial imagination had not yet recovered the legal grammar of incorporation.

This is made all the more clear in the transposing of *sanguis testamenti* for *sanguis foederis*, a subtle but telling shift by Lancelot Andrewes in his invention of a "covenant of peace." As he explains:

> 'Two powers were in it: I. as sanguis foederis, 'the blood of the covenant,' the covenant of peace, for in blood were the covenants

made; that with Abraham in Genesis fifteen, that with Moses, in Exodus twenty-four, in blood both....'[92]

Unfortunately, he will not be the last to invent a theological covenant that supersedes those entrusted to the prophets and ratified in blood.

The tragedy is that the enmity remained, it was not slain. The tragedy is that the commonwealth of Israel, once juridically real, was rendered allegorical, like a vanished kingdom in a medieval romance. The blood was real (*sanguis foederis*), but the polity was fictionalized (*sanguis testamenti*). Andrewes, in his brilliance, transposed the terms, but in doing so, he re-scripted the covenant as a liturgical abstraction rather than a legal incorporation.

It is Hamlet's Denmark: the rightful heir returns, the poison is purged, but the throne is ceded to Fortinbras. The reconciliation occurs, but the inheritance is lost. It is no wonder that so many have sought solace in historical fiction looking for the split in Sangreal.

The textual failure is not merely a matter of oversight, it is a theological fracture. The refusal to connect the mediator of Exodus 24 with that of Matthew 26:28, Mark 14:24, and Luke 22:20 is not accidental; it is codified. The Synod of Dordt, in its pronouncement, institutionalized a rupture between covenantal ratification and sacrificial mediation. It declared—without tremor—that the purpose of Christ's death was not to establish in actual fact a new covenant of grace by His blood, but merely to acquire for the Father the right to re-enter covenantal dialogue. A juridical permission, not a covenantal enactment. This is not exegesis, it is evasion. It conflicts directly with the testimony of Scripture, which declares that Christ became the guarantor and mediator of a better covenant (Hebrews 7:22; 9:15), not one that leaves the reader asking which one He became, or that a will, a covenant, comes into force only through death. The blood of Christ is not a legal possibility; it is the ratifying medium. The covenant is not potential, it is enacted. And this failure was not confined to the

Synod. The Synod of Dordt commissioned what would become the *Statenvertaling,* the "States Translation", as the first official Dutch Bible rendered directly from the sacred tongues. Published in 1637, it bore the imprimatur of ecclesial authority and linguistic fidelity, anchoring the Dutch Reformed tradition in Scripture. It selectively deployed terms like verbond, verbinden, maken, gemaakt, testament, and middelaar, each chosen not for fidelity to the Hebrew or Greek, but for theological convenience. The Authorized Version did the same. Both translations treated conflation as a hermeneutic. Just who is supposed to die here becomes a theological mess. This is not just a mistranslation, it is a mislocation of meaning. The mediator of Exodus 24 stood in blood. The mediator of Matthew 26 did the exact same. To sever them is to sever the covenant itself.

The problem isn't just a bad translation, it's a deep misunderstanding. Scripture shows that covenants are made through blood, not theory. Moses stood in blood at Sinai; Jesus did the same at the Last Supper. But later theologians and translators split that connection, treating Christ's death as permission for God to make a covenant, that is devoid of content, the purpose of which the theologians get to play, fill in the blanks. Really, just look at the text of the Statenvertaling.

JEREMIA 31

Oude Testament De profeet:
31 Ziet, de dagen komen, spreekt de HEERE, dat Ik met het huis van Israel en met het huis van Juda een nieuw **verbond** zal **maken**; 32 Niet naar het **verbond**, dat Ik met hun vaderen **gemaakt** heb, ten dage als Ik hun hand aangreep, om hen uit Egypteland uit te voeren, welk Mijn verbond zij vernietigd hebben, hoewel Ik hen getrouwd had, spreekt de HEERE; 33 Maar dit is het **verbond**, dat Ik na die dagen met het huis van Israel **maken** zal, spreekt de HEERE: Ik zal Mijn wet in hun binnenste geven, en zal die in hun hart schrijven; en Ik zal hun tot een God zijn, en zij zullen Mij tot een volk zijn.

34 En zij zullen niet meer, een iegelijk zijn naaste, en een iegelijk
zijn broeder, leren, zeggende: Kent den HEERE! want zij zullen
Mij allen kennen, van hun kleinste af tot hun grootste toe, spreekt
de HEERE; want Ik zal hun ongerechtigheid vergeven, en hunner
zonden niet meer gedenken.

HEBREEËN 8

De brief van de apostel Paulus aan de:
8 Want hen berispende, zegt Hij tot hen: Ziet, de dagen komen,
spreekt de Heere, en Ik zal over het huis Israels, en over het huis
van Juda een nieuw **verbond** oprichten;
9 Niet naar het verbond, dat Ik met hun vaderen **gemaakt** heb, ten
dage, als Ik hen bij de hand nam, om hen uit Egypteland te leiden;
want zij zijn in dit Mijn **verbond** niet gebleven, en Ik heb op hen
niet geacht, zegt de Heere.
10 Want dit is het **verbond**, dat Ik met het huis Israels **maken** zal
na die dagen, zegt de Heere: Ik zal Mijn wetten in hun verstand
geven, en in hun harten zal Ik die inschrijven; en Ik zal hun tot een
God zijn, en zij zullen Mij tot een volk zijn.

**On the Lexical Discrepancy in Statenvertaling's Covenant Termi-
nology**

Having the official Statenvertaling renderings of *Jeremiah 31* and
Hebrews 8 before us, we are immediately confronted with the lexical
triad: **verbond, gemaakt,** and **maken**. These choices, while canonized
in Dutch ecclesial tradition, demand scrutiny. They point us not
merely to theological interpretation but to the lexicon itself, a Dutch
lexicon, yes, but one that must be interrogated through the lens of Hebrew covenantal idiom.

Dr. Pieter J. Hoedemaker encapsulates the translation mandate
with striking clarity:

"De opdracht was duidelijk: blijf zo dicht mogelijk bij de Hebreeuwse tekst! Mocht hierdoor geen helder Nederlands ontstaan, dan diende er in de kanttekeningen een duidelijke uitleg te worden gegeven."[93]

This statement, while noble in intent, exposes a **conundrum**. The verbs **gemaakt** and **maken,** used to describe the divine act of covenant, fail to reflect the Hebrew כָּרַת (*karat*), which unambiguously means "to cut." The theological weight of *cutting a covenant* is not semantic ornamentation, it is **ritual ontology**, bound to blood, sacrifice, and irrevocable bond.

That the translators appear to have equated maken with snijden is not merely a lexical oversight, it is a hermeneutical fracture. Why *snijden, or in past tense would be sneed (singular) or sneden (plural),* was not employed remains a problem for the contextually rigorous minds of Johannes Bogerman, Willem Baudartius, and Gerson Bucerus, the triad commissioned for the *Tenach.* Likewise, the Apostolic corpus entrusted to Jacobus Rolandus, Hermannus Faukelius, Petrus Cornelisz, Festus Hommius, and Antonius Walaeus, suffers from the same lexical flattening.

The omission of *snijden* is not a mere linguistic choice, it is a theological dilution. And for those of us committed to restoring covenantal meaning with typographic and semantic fidelity, this is not a footnote. It is a call to re-render, re-annotate, and re-illuminate.

The Confessional Witness to Covenant Structure and Terminology

This established view, that covenant is not merely a theological abstraction but a ritually grounded, lexically precise bond, finds confessional expression across the Reformed tradition. The following documents, each bearing the weight of ecclesial authority and exegetical rigor, articulate this framework with striking consistency:

1. **Westminster Confession of Faith (1646)[94]**
   a. **Chapter VII, p4**   'in reference to the death of Jesus Christ

the testator,'
    b. **Chapter VIII, p7** 'Christ, in the work of mediation,'
    c. **Chapter XIX, p3** 'All which ceremonial laws are now
    abrogated under the New Testament.'

2. **Savoy Declaration of Faith and Order (1658)[95]**
    a. **Chapter VII, p4** 'the death of Jesus Christ the testator,'
    b. **Chapter VIII, p7** 'Christ in the work of mediation acteth
    according to both natures'
    c. **Chapter XIX, p3** 'ceremonial laws being appointed only to
    the time of reformation'
    d. **Chapter XX,** *p4* 'the gospel be the only outward means of
    revealing Christ'

3. **London Baptist Confession of Faith (1677/1689)[96]**
    a. **Chapter VIII, p7** 'Christ, in the work of mediation, acteth
    according to both natures'
    b. **Chapter XIX, p3** 'for that end abrogated and taken away.'
    c. **Chapter XX, p4** 'the gospel be the only outward means of
    revealing Christ'

Shakespeare's admonition *to thine own self be true* was on display in
the Westminster Assembly, which emerged not from ecclesial consensus but from the theological tensions that shaped its formation. The
positions of James and Charles regarding episcopacy stood in direct
conflict with the presbyterians, the congregationalists, and the Eras-
tians commissioned by the Long Parliament. Charles refused to autho-
rize the attendance of the episcopalians. How each faction understood
its own ecclesial identity is further evidenced in Chapter XIV, part 1
of the Confession.

None of these confessions resolved the sacerdotal implications of
the sacraments. B. B. Warfield makes this clear, devoting an entire section to the unresolved tensions within part 2 of his assessment. The

Westminster Standards did not address the problem of *partaken of* sacraments as a *dispensatio* of propitiatory sacrifice. That theological architecture was already established in the Augsburg Confession.

The English Civil War and the Thirty Years' War were not answers to the biblical text. Singing the words of James R. Lowell's poem, set to music by Thomas J. Williams, though anachronistic and strikingly appropriate, is not the answer either. The resolution of the Treaty of Westphalia did not offer a better answer to the question of who we are. That answer is found only in the fulfillment of Jeremiah chapter thirty-one.

Finally, the question must be asked, did the hymns of the time reflect the covenantal continuity of the prophetic word and its fulfillment in the message of the Kingdom of God, or merely the theology of the day? Was the proper understanding of Mediation for a covenant ever truly expressed in the verse and song of this period? One must turn to one of the most prolific hymnists, Charles Wesley (1707–1788), whose corpus, some six thousand hymns, is often held as sufficient evidence of theological depth. Yet within these volumes, only three hymns employ the word *covenant*, and none invoke *mediator*.

Hymns with Covenant—A Brief Catalogue of Absence[97]
1. The New Covenant stanza 1
2. Thy covenant this, that I shall know stanza 1
3. He will ever be mindful of his covenant a subheading of a short hymn.

This absence is not incidental, it is symptomatic. How is it that neither the theology nor the song of this period could reflect the individual or communal belonging that covenant demands? How could they fail to exhibit our standing, our fellowship, our being *in Him*? The silence is not poetic, it is theological.

So how are we to harmonize this with the covenant in which we belong to Him, the *karat*, the cutting, the binding, the blood-sealed promise? If the hymns do not sing it, and the theology does not support it, then we must render it anew, typographically, theologically, and liturgically. The covenant must be seen, sung. Anything less is a dissonance we must resolve.

Eight

❦

Constructed Reality

'There has always been a hermeneutic problem in Christianity because Christianity proceeds from a proclamation' - Paul Ricoeur

Paul Ricoeur's accusation is certainly not a phenomenon. It is a symptom, a hermeneutical rupture that has metastasized across centuries. Has the last two thousand years laid out traditions that override Scriptural context becoming the hermeneutic? Undeniably. The chapters in this book have not merely traced that drift, they have catalogued a massive poleptic. A reckoning.

Paul, not to be confused with Shaul, has become the strawman of theology. So many words put into his mouth. Not the apostle, but the construct. The ecclesial Paul. The Pauline cipher installed in the chancellorship of Antiochian and Alexandrian schools, where covenantal fidelity is reduced into doctrinal abstraction. This is illustrated by a recent conversation I had about the nativity of 'Jesus'. I asked: If we knew the date of Jesus' birth should we honor him on that day. The reply was "We don't know the real date, so any date will do, so long as it's December 25th." This is emblematic of where we are at today. We are living in a world where symbol has outlived substance, and where ritual, identity, and irony have become the framework for meaning, even when the original covenantal architecture has collapsed or been forgotten.

The phrase "Messy-Antics" a pun on *Messianic,* emerged as a satirical critique from within the Messianic movement itself. It's not an academic term, but a grassroots neologism coined to express frustration with what some see as theological confusion, performative Torah observance, or sensationalism in parts of the movement. One of the earliest documented

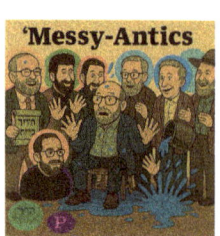

Messianics

uses comes from a personal reflection published by Torah Resources "My friend Aaron just called 'Messianic', *Messi-Antics.*". This play on words Messianic → Messi-Antics was used to highlight the perceived antics, drama, or doctrinal inconsistency that had crept into some corners of the movement.

Is this the community implied by Yeshua? Do any of these ecclesial constructs, be they denominational, Messianic, or para-liturgical, actually represent the House of Israel and the House of Judah, from which He emerged as the *one from the flock,* the lamb Yochanan declared with covenantal finality?

Yeshua's halachic dictums were not ornamental, they were instructional. His invocation of the Seat of Moshe in *Matthew 23:2,* paired with the imperative τηρειτε και ποιειτε ("observe and do"), has suffered too many objections from those who prefer theological abstraction over covenantal obedience.

We all recognize that *Matthew 5:18* "until heaven and earth pass away..." is most faithfully cited not in a lecture hall, but at a sunrise service, where the Torah's permanence is felt in the breath and light of creation itself.

This view of Torah is not theoretical, it is on full display in Yeshua's confrontation with the Perushim, not the Tzedukim. The issue was not what they taught, but what they failed to do. That is the point. The

Church, in its post-Pauline architecture, has made Torah observance the problem, not the solution.

The invocation of *II Corinthians 3:6* "the letter kills, but the Spirit gives life" as a superlative rule that allows interpretation to override covenantal fidelity has become foundational to Western hermeneutics. It is the cornerstone of counter-missionary rhetoric, and Rabbinic Judaism, tragically, is complicit in maintaining this strawman, a caricature of Torah as burden, rather than as ratified instruction.

So how is II Timothy 2:15 not a hermeneutical problem? Look at the verse. The phrase *"rightly dividing"*—often quoted, rarely interrogated—is not a doctrinal triumph but a theological trap. The Greek ορθοτομουντα is not benign; it forms the objective clause of τηρειτε και ποιειτε in 2 Timothy 2:16. The implication is clear: misdivision leads to ungodliness. This is not a call to precision—it's a warning against fragmentation.

Dispensational interpreters treat "rightly dividing" as a license to partition Scripture into epochs, covenants, and categories that fracture the unity of Torah and the testimony of Yeshua. But the verse itself resists such slicing. It demands fidelity, not segmentation.

Scott J. Hafemann names the trap. In section 3 of his introduction to *The Letter/Spirit Contrast*, he cites Kamlah, Käsemann, and Stuhlmacher—not to reinforce the dichotomy, but to expose its theological cost. The hermeneutical problem isn't just misreading—it's the structural avoidance of what Exodus 19:9 declares with covenantal clarity:

> "Then the LORD said to Moses, 'Behold, I will come to you in a thick cloud, so that the people may hear when I speak with you and may also trust in you forever.'"

It is the latter clause, **וְגַם בְּךָ יַאֲמִינוּ לְעוֹלָם**, that modern theology cannot metabolize. The LORD did not say Moshe would be temporarily relevant. He said Moshe would be trusted *forever*. That is death to any theology that seeks to set Moses aside, whether through Pauline misreadings or post-Enlightenment abstraction.

Moshe is not a placeholder. He is the ratified voice through whom the covenant was heard, and through whom trust was established. Any hermeneutic worth its ink must reinforce that trust—not divide it.

Currently, there's a growing constellation of authors and pop-theological voices orbiting the Messianic Community, some on the perimeter, others embedded within. Such men as Monte Judah, Joseph Good, Nehemia Gordon, Dr. Ron Moseley, Daniel Lancaster, Sid Roth, Chuck Pierce, Dr. Mark Blitz, and Dr. Baruch Korman. On the outside, we have figures like N.T. Wright and Michael Heiser, they could be associated with such predecessors as Willaim Beveridge. both of whom carry solid academic credentials and have contributed mean-ingfully to biblical scholarship, even if their frameworks diverge from covenantal restoration. Their work deserves engagement, not dis-missal. The late Michael Heiser was

Then there are those operating within the Messianic and Charis-matic spheres Perry Stone, Jonathan Cahn, Rabbi Jonathan Bernis, Dr. Michael Brown, and Bill Cloud. Each has carved out a platform, each is successful by conventional metrics: book sales, media presence, and audience reach. But success alone is not the measure. The question remains: *Are they restoring the sanctity of the text, or repackaging it for consumption?* That's where typographic fidelity, semantic nuance, and covenantal clarity must be brought to bear.

The late Michael Heiser's hermeneutical reset, a call to abandon modern assumptions and re-enter the ancient Hebraic worldview in which Scripture was birthed. Heiser first popularized this in *The Bible Unfiltered*, where he writes:

> "But you must remember that, while the Bible was written for us, it wasn't written to us."[98]

Michael Heiser possessed an encyclopedic command of biblical languages, ancient Near Eastern contexts, and theological frameworks, his scholarship spanned disciplines with rare precision. For all his scholarly prowess, Heiser's persistent use of the term "Testament" felt like a hermeneutical dissonance, a lexical holdover that undermined his otherwise Hebraic recalibration. It may have been tactical, perhaps a concession to evangelical familiarity, but it risked reinforcing the very supersessionist framework he so often dismantled elsewhere.

What Jonathan Cahn is actually promoting is not exegesis but a theatrical hermenuetic masquerading as revelation. His method redefines interpretation to mean the propagation of false analogies, *post hoc ergo propter hoc* fallacies, circular reasoning, confirmation bias, non sequitur, and most egregiously, the incessant appeal to Mystery as a substitute for textual fidelity. One has to ask if this appeal originated with FrontLine or Charisma House? He bypasses covenantal context, flattens semantic nuance, that is, he oversimplifies the meaning of the words, ignoring the deeper layers or specific details that make them powerful or unique, and treats typology as a marketing device rather than a theological scaffold.

Cahn's rush to publish, complete with cinematic trailers and apocalyptic branding, suggests that drama is not the byproduct of his message but the mechanism by which he justifies it. The sacred text becomes a stage prop, and the exegete becomes a showman. What's lost in the spectacle is the integrity of the manuscript, the reverence of covenantal meaning, and the discipline of true exegesis.

Though I do sympathize with his promotion of a Hebraic understanding of the Scriptures and Prophetic issues, that sympathy does not extend to the methods by which he distorts the text to fit a narrative. The restoration of meaning demands reverence, not theatrics.

Bibliography

1. Aquinas, Thomas — Summa Theologica
2. Barr, James — The Semantics of Biblical Language
3. Bede — Ecclessiastical History of England
4. Calvin, John — Institutes of the Christian Religion
5. Carrol, Lewis — Alice's Adventures in Wonderland
6. Gruber, Daniel — The Seperation of Church and Faith
7. Gruber, Daniel — The Church and the Jews
8. Hafeman, Scott J. — Paul, Moses, and the History of Israel
9. Miller, Duane D. — The Messiah According to Moses in the Scroll of the Torah
10. Nanos, Mark — Mystery of Romans
11. Ryrie, Charles Caldwell — Dispensationalism Today
12. Shakespeare, William — Twelfth Night
13. Terry, Milton S. — Biblical Hermenuetics
14. Zetterholm, Magnus — The Formation of Christianity in Antioch
15. Shulam, Joseph — Hidden Treasures
16. Davidson, Benjamin — The Analytical Hebrew and Chaldee Lexicon
17. Hegg, Tim — The Letter Writer
18. Stern, David H. — Messianic Jewish Manifesto
19. Parks, Jerry — False Security
20. Lancaster, D. Thomas — Restoration
21. Walvoord, John F. — The Millennial Kingdom
22. Nash, Ronald H. — Christianity & the Hellenistic World
23. Skarsuane, Oskar — Mishkan

Articles

Articles

End Notes

Chapter One:

1. How New Was Paul's Gospel? Sheffield Academic Press 1994
2. Ibid
3. the genitive declension supplements the article in translation
4. Dispensationalism Today, Charles Caldwell Ryrie, Moody Press, chapter 1, page 15
5. Ibid, page 15
6. Ibid, page 16
7. George E. Mendenhall, "Covenant Forms in Israelite Tradition", The Biblical Archaeologist 17 (Sept 1954), pp 50-76
8. Law and Covenant in Israel and the Ancient Near East, Part II, page 3, Mendenhall
9. Korosec
10. Joshua A. Berman's "God's Alliance with Man" article in Azure no, 25 Summer 5766/2006
11. 'Hethitische Staatsvertrage' by T. Weicher 1931
12. Ibid
13. The Seperation of Church and Faith: Copernicus and the Jews, Daniel Gruber, chapter 4
14. What is the New Covenant "Law" in Jeremiah 31:33? Published in Bibliotheca sacra, 163, no. 651 J1-S 2006, pp 312-321

Chapter Two

15. Perseus Project: http://perseus.tufts.edu/hopper/

16. Scott W. Hahn 'A Broken Covenant and the Curse of Death: A Study of Hebrew'

17. Perseus Digital Library Project Ed. Gregory R. Crane, Tufts University.

18. op. cit & 8 ibid

19. op. cit. & 8 ibid

20. Ibid [16]

21. The Semantics of Biblical Language, Oxford University Press, 1961

22. Paul and Palestinian Judaism 1977 SCM Press

23. The Seperation of Church and Faith: Copernicus and the Jews, Daniel Gruber Elijah Publishing, PO Box 776 Hanover, NH 03755, chapter 3, section 1, pp 42-43

24. Biblical Hermeneutics by Milton S. Terry, S.T. D., 1883, Phillips & Hunt, Part III - History of Biblical Interpretation, Chapter 1 Ancient Jewish Exegesis, p. 614

Chapter Three

25. Twelth Night, Act 3, Scene 4

26. The Formation of Christianity in Antioch, chapter 1, p.3

27. Shulchan Aruch, chapter 246: The Laws of Lending and Renting to a Gentile on the Sabbath: section 4

28. The Complete Artscroll Siddur (Nusach Sefard) pp. 16,17

29. The Apostolic Fathers Greek Texts and English Translations of Their Writings - Baker Book House Company 1992

30. www.opentext.org/

31. www.inthebeginning.org/

32. Bible Knowledge Commentary: Colossians, p. 678,

33. this is the Greek equvilant to OPPS

34. Ibid

35. Letter to the Philadelphians 8

36. Magnesians: Chapter 8

37. Essay "The Covenant Idea in Irenaeus of Lyons: An Introduction and Survey - Confessing Our Hope Essays in Honor of Morton Howison Smith on His Eightieth Birthday by Joseph A Pipa, Jr and C.N. Willborn, Chapter 2, pp 43-45

38. http://www.ccel.org

39. op. cit.,

40. AH 4.2.3 'TheWritings of Moses ar the words of Christ'

41. http://www.newadvent.org

Chapter Four

42. Post-Nicene Fathers series, Volume VI: The Writings of Jerome. Patrologia Latina

43. http://www.newadvent.org/fathers/1102.htm

44. Jerome, Prologue to Jeremiah

45. http://penelope.uchicago.edu

46. The Separation of Church & Faith: Copernicus and the Jews, Elijah Publishing 2005, p. 42

Chapter Five

47. Dogmatic Treatises, Against Eunomius, Book II, part 12, 3-4

48. Dogmatic Treatises, Against Eunomius, Book IV, part 8, 15-16

49. the 'making divine' or the deification of an earthly entity, namely a group, or activity.

50. Regula S.P.N. Benedict

51. 'by patience share in the sufferings of Christ, and in the kingdom so that we may deserve to come to share in his'

52. Isidore of Seville. *Etymologiae.* Book V, Chapter 24. *The Latin Library*, https://www.thelatinlibrary.com/isidore/5.shtml

53. Isidore of Seville. *Etymologiae.* Book V, Chapter 24. *The Latin Library*,

54. Ibid

55. *Beda Venerabilis, Historia Ecclesiastica Gentis Anglorum*, Liber III, Caput XXIX. Latin text available via The Perseus Digital Library

56. *Ibid*

57. Thomas Aquinas, *Summa Theologiae*, III^a q. 78 a. 1 arg. In: *Sancti Thomae Aquinatis Opera Omnia*, ed. Leonina, vol. 12.

58. Thomas Aquinas, *Summa Theologiae*, I–II, q. 107, a. 1, arg. 2

59. Wyclif, John. *On the Truth of Holy Scripture*. Translated with introduction and notes by Ian Christopher Levy. Kalamazoo, MI: Medieval Institute Publications, 2001.

60. Bruce, F. F. "John Wycliffe and the English Bible." *Churchman* 98, no. 4 (1984): 308–319.

61. *Sir Gawain and the Green Knight*. Edited by J.R.R. Tolkien, E.V. Gordon, and Norman Davis, 2nd ed., Oxford University Press, 1967. Lines 2330–2350.

62. Ibid

63. Corpus Christi College, Cambridge, MS 140. Anglo-Saxon Gospels (West Saxon dialect), ca. 1000. Traditionally attributed to Ælfric of Eynsham.

64. https://www.textusreceptusbibles.com/Wessex/

Chapter Six

65. Alice in Wonderland

66. Monty Python, The Last Supper, performed by Eric Idle and John Cleese, in Monty Python Live at the Hollywood Bowl, UK Columbia Pictures, 1982

67. Calvin, John. *Institutes of the Christian Religion*. Translated by Henry Beveridge. Grand Rapids: Eerdmans, 1989. Book I, Chapter V, Section 7.

68. Calvin, John. *Institutes of the Christian Religion*. Translated by Henry Beveridge, Christian Classics Ethereal Library, Book II, Chapter 9, Section 2.

69. Institutes of the Christian Religion: Book II, chapter 9,part 3

70. Calvin, J. (n.d.). *Institutes of the Christian Religion* (H. Beveridge, Trans.). Christian Classics Ethereal Library. Book II, Chapter 7, Section 3. Retrieved August 28, 2025

71. "Epistle 695" in *Collected Works of Erasmus Vol. 5: Letters 594 to 841, 1517–1518* (tr. R.A.B. Mynors and D.F.S. Thomson; annotated by James K. McConica; Toronto: University of Toronto Press, 1976), 172.

72. https://atwistedcrownofthorns.com/2012/08/26/william-tyndale/

73. William Tyndale, quoted in Herbert Samworth, "The Life of William Tyndale – Part 15," *Tyndale's Ploughboy*, March 5, 2019.

74. https://biblehub.com/tyndale/hebrews/8.htm

75. David , *The Bible in English*, p. 147

76. Tyndale, William. *An Answer to Sir Thomas More's Dialogue*. 1531. *The Works of William Tyndale*, edited by Henry Walter, Cambridge University Press, 1848, p. 307.

77. Ibid

78. Hahn, Scott W. "A Broken Covenant and the Curse of Death: A Study of Hebrews 9:15–22." *The Catholic Biblical Quarterly*, vol. 66, no. 3, 2004, p. 416.

Chapter Seven

79. Carroll, Lewis. *Alice's Adventures in Wonderland*. 1865. Chapter XII: Alice's Evidence. Lit2Go Edition.

80. Henry Gee and William John Hardy, eds., *Documents Illustrative of English Church History* (New York: Macmillan, 1896), 508–511.

81. Ibid

82. Gee, Henry, and William John Hardy, eds. *Documents Illustrative of English Church History*. Macmillan, 1896, pp. 508–511.

83. William Shakespeare's **Hamlet, Act 2, Scene 2**

84. Gee, Henry, and William John Hardy, eds. *Documents Illustrative of English Church History*. London: Macmillan, 1896, pp. 523–525.

85. Tyndale, William. *The New Testament Translated by William Tyndale, 1534 Edition*. Edited by David Daniell, Yale University Press, 1989, p. xii (Prologue).

86. Shim, Jai-Sung. *Biblical Hermeneutics and Hebraism in the Early Seventeenth Century as Reflected in the Work of John Weemse (1579–1636)*. Ph.D. Dissertation, Calvin Theological Seminary, 1998.

87. Shim, Jai-Sung. *Biblical Hermeneutics and Hebraism in the Early Seventeenth Century as Reflected in the Work of John Weemse (1579–1636)*. Ph.D. Dissertation, Calvin Theological Seminary, 1998.

88. Weemse, John. *Exercitations Divine: Containing Diverse Questions and Solutions for the Right Understanding of the Scriptures*. London: Printed by M. Flesher for R. Dawlman, 1632.

89. Weemse, John. *The Christian Synagogue: Wherein Is Contained the Diverse Reading, the Right Pointing, Translation, and Collation of Scripture with Scripture. With the Customes of the Hebrewes and Proselytes, and of All Those Nations with Whom They Were Conversant. Digested into Three Bookes*. London: Printed by John Dawson and George Eld for John Bellamie, 1623.

90. Lightfoot Volume XI, Chapter 21.24.19 VI, Luke 22

91. Beveridge, William. *The Works of the Right Reverend Father in God, William Beveridge, D.D.* Vol. 6, Parker, 1842.

92. Lancelot Andrewes, *Apospasmatia Sacra: Or A Collection of Posthumous and Orphan Lectures*, London: R. Norton for Richard Royston, 1657.

93. Pieter J. Hoedemaker,

94. Westminster Assembly. *The Westminster Confession of Faith: With Proof Texts*. Horsham, PA: Great Commission Publications, 1992.

95. Savoy Assembly. *The Savoy Declaration of Faith and Order, 1658*. Reprint, Glasgow: Free Presbyterian Publications, 1998.

96. Baptist Elders and Brethren. *The Second London Baptist Confession of Faith, 1677/1689*. Reprint. Pensacola, FL: Chapel Library, n.d.

97. https://expositorysongs.com/songwriter/charles-wesley/

Chapter Eight

98. Heiser, Michael S. 2017. *The Bible Unfiltered: Approaching Scripture on Its Own Terms*. Bellingham, WA: Lexham Press.

Testamentum

The invaluable dictionary by William Smith, D.C.L., LL.D.: is a must read for those seeking an understanding of Testamentum,

He states that a TESTAMENTUM is "mentis nostrae justa contestatio in id solemniter facta ut post mortem valeat" He goes on to state the order by which a Roman will is valid. The term for which this validity is considered to be legal is the Testator must have 'Testamentifactio'.

There were three ways in which a will could be made. The first being Calata Comitia, the second being In Procinctu, the third being Testamentum. The issue to be understood is that Yeshua, not being of a particular class of Roman citizen was prohibited by Law from making Testamentum.

See the Article by George Long, M.A., Fellow of Trinity College on pp 1113 - 1118

The Lost Hermenuetic

Does a Biblical hermeneutic contain a purpose that is stated by the LORD? Yes, and it is not speculative. It is stated. It is covenantal. It is functional. Hermeneutics are not an end in themselves; they are a means of alignment, a tool of fidelity. The LORD does not call for interpretive gymnastics, He calls for covenantal obedience, rightly divided and rightly embodied.

We are not left without textual scaffolding. Two passages, not exclusive to any sectarian group, speak directly to this:

- II Timothy 2:15–16: *"Be diligent to present yourself approved to God, a worker who does not need to be ashamed, rightly dividing the word of truth. But shun profane and vain babblings..."* This is not a call to cleverness. It is a call to craftsmanship. The verb ορθοτομουντα, to cut straight, evokes covenantal precision, not theological abstraction. The worker is not praised for novelty, but for fidelity.
- John 5:46: *"For if you believed Moses, you would believe Me; for he wrote about Me."* This is not a metaphor. It is a hermeneutic of continuity. The Messiah affirms that Moses' writings are not merely historical, they are prophetic, Christological, covenantal. The interpretive act must be tethered to divine authorship and messianic fulfillment.

And we begin even earlier. Devarim (Deuteronomy) 4:2:

ולא תגרעו ממנו לשמר את מצות יהוה אלהיכם

"You shall not add to the word which I command you, nor take from it..." This is the boundary of hermeneutics. The LORD sets the perimeter. The interpreter is not a legislator. He is a steward. The text is not raw material for theological construction, it is sacred architecture, already designed.

So yes, the Biblical hermeneutic contains a purpose. It is stated by the LORD. It is covenantal in origin, messianic in fulfillment, and guarded by textual integrity. We do not interpret to innovate. We interpret to obey.

The Imperative of Divine Speech: Hermeneutic Boundaries and Covenantal Relevance

Similar expressions of textual inviolability are not scattered, they are strategically placed. They form a perimeter around the sanctity of divine utterance:

- Deuteronomy 12:32: *"You shall not add to it or take from it."*

- Proverbs 30:6: *"Do not add to His words, lest He rebuke you and you be found a liar."*
- Revelation 22:18–19: *"If anyone adds… if anyone takes away…"*

These are not literary flourishes. They are covenantal guardrails. The LORD does not permit editorial license. He demands fidelity.

This is not merely a textual concern, it is a matter of life. Matthew 4:4 and Luke 4:4 do not present dietary metaphors. They declare existential dependence:

"Man shall not live by bread alone, but by every word that proceeds from the mouth of God." The clause εκπορευομενω δια στοματος θεου is not poetic, it is procedural. It defines the mechanism of life itself. The Word is not supplemental, it is elemental.

Now consider **John 5:46–47**. Verse 46 affirms:

"For if you believed Moses, you would believe Me; for he wrote about Me." Verse 47 follows with a conditional: *"But if you do not believe his writings, how will you believe My words?"* The verb -

(imperfect active indicative, 2nd person plural) implies ongoing entrustment. It is not a one-time assent—it is a sustained covenantal posture. The rhetorical "if" is not dismissive, it is diagnostic. It exposes the fracture between professed belief and textual submission.

Thus, the denial of Moshe's authority is not academic, it is covenantal rebellion. It is a rejection of the very mechanism by which life is sustained:

"But on every word that comes out of the mouth of God." (Matthew 4:4b)

There is no uninspirational clause in Scripture. No procedural footnote. No divine filler. There is no mechanism by which His Word becomes not His Word. Every utterance is covenantal infrastructure. This is substantiated in Sh'mot (Exodus) 19:9:

"And the LORD said to Moses, 'Behold, I come to you in a thick cloud, that the people may hear when I speak with you, and believe you forever.'" God's speaking to Moshe is not ambient, it is in the matter of permanent witness. It is the structure of prophetic legitimacy. It is the auditory covenant that binds the people to the prophet and the prophet to the Word.

So in fact Paul did guard the Word. He is demonstrating that he, in practice, was upholding or guarding the Word. He was in line with Deuteronomy 4:6

Scripture References

Book	Verse(s)	Page	Book	Verse(s)	Page
Bereshiet	6:9	57	Bereshiet	6:18	56
Bereshiet	6:20	56	Beresheit	9	56
Bereshiet	9:8	56	Bereshiet	9:9	56
Bereshiet	9:10	56	Bereshiet	15	141
Bereshiet	9:12	56	Bereshiet	12:49	58
Sh'mot	19:9	23, 24, 25, 166, 180	Sh'mot	9:12	40, 42
Sh'mot	24	40, 43, 44, 45	Sh'mot	24:3-11	44, 45
Sh'mot	24:4	45	Sh'mot	24:5-6	40
Sh'mot	24:11	45	Sh'mot	24:8	41, 42, 46
Sh'mot	24:11	45	Vayikra	24:22	58

Yeramiyahu	31:34	115, 140, 141	Yeramiyahu	38:31	11, 12, 15, 2
Y'cheskel	40	9	Y'cheskel	43:18	49
Y'cheskel	48	9			
Amos	9:11	60	Zechariyah	8:23	60
Tehelim	22:27	60	Tehelim	82:6	107
Tehelim	119:152	22, 23	Mati	4:4	180
Mati	5:17	53, 54	Mati	23:2	16 5
Mati	23:3	72,	Mati	26:28	11, 12, 15
Markom	14:24	11, 12, 125, 157	Lukam	1:72	96, 125
Lukam	22:20	6, 11, 12, 125, 157	Lukam	24:44	78
Yochanan	5:46	134, 179	Yochanan	5:46, 47	180
Acts	5:17	53	Acts	15	53, 59, 62, 77

Greek Lexica Targets

Both the Septuagint and the Apostolic writings summon the lexica, not as mere reference tools, but as witnesses to the semantic structure behind covenantal transmission. These texts do not merely cite words; they encode theological architecture. To perform this analysis faithfully, the most robust and transparent resource is the **Perseus Project of Tufts University** (www.perseus.tufts.edu), which allows us to trace lexical strata across Classical and Koine Greek with manuscript fidelity.

To reconstruct what transpired linguistically, we must first catalog every term that could have been employed in rendering covenantal intent. This includes not only the source words:

- בְּרִית **(Brit)**   covenant
- כָּרַת **(Karat)**   to cut, to ratify

...but also their target equivalents in Greek.

I. Words for Covenant
These six terms form the semantic constellation of covenantal meaning:

a. **βουλομαι** , to will, to intend b. **διαθηκη** , covenant, testament c. **συμβολαιον** , contract, compact d. **διαλλαγη** , reconciliation e. **ορκον** , oath f. **συνθηκη**, agreement, treaty

Each term carries distinct theological and legal nuance, and must be weighed not only by lexical definition but by contextual deployment in LXX and NT passages.

II. Ratifying Verbs
Next, we trace the ratifying source term, the Hebrew verb that seals or enacts the covenant, and its Greek counterparts. This is not merely a lexical exercise; it is a restoration of intent. The ratification verb, whether כָּרַת or its sacrificial analogues, must be mapped to Greek terms such as:

a. **διατιθημι** , to establish, to set forth b. **ποιεω** , to make, to do c. **τελεω** , to complete, to fulfill d. **συντιθημι** , to agree, to compact e. **συνθηκη** , agreement (noun form) f. **κυροω** , to ratify, to confirm g. **σφραγιζω** , to seal, h,. **κόπτω**, to *to strike, cut, or sever.*

These verbs are not interchangeable. Each encodes a different mode of covenantal enactment, some sacrificial, some legal, some relational. Their deployment across manuscripts reveals the intentional architecture of divine-human engagement.

Only by assembling this full lexical constellation, source and target, noun and verb, oath and seal, can we begin to visualize the covenantal framework as it was rendered, received, and ratified across languages and traditions. This is not just translation, it is semantic restoration.

I am going to argue, without apology, that true translation is not the art of convenience, but the discipline of restoration. If the target language lacks a cognate, then the translator must introduce a new word or concept, one that maintains the original intent rather than degrading it. This is inherently difficult. But translating sacred text is difficult. It should be.

To simply choose the word with the closest meaning may feel expedient, but it is a semantic shortcut that misleads the reader. It trades fidelity for familiarity, and in doing so, it distorts the covenantal structure encoded in the source.

If your intent is to manipulate understanding, to steer interpretation through lexical sleight, then you are not preserving the Word of the LORD. You are reframing it. And that is not translation. That is theological trespass.

Covenants of Promise

Covenants of Promise

JON M LOOSE

Author's Note

Author's Note: These have been the ramblings of a layman, uncredentialed, uninitiated, and without formal education. What I lack in academic pedigree I've tried to make up for in fidelity, curiosity, and a refusal to let consensus flatten the sacred. If anything here proves useful, it's by grace, not qualification.

www.ingramcontent.com/pod-product-compliance
Lightning Source LLC
Chambersburg PA
CBHW051515120626
46551CB00012B/936